the SELF LOVE WORKBOOK FOR TEENS

A Transformative Guide to Boost Self-Esteem, Build Healthy Mindsets, and Embrace Your True Self

Shainna Ali, PhD

Published in the United States by:
Ulysses Press
P. O. Box 3440
Berkeley, CA 94703
www.ulyssespress.com

ISBN: 978-1-64604-0100
Library of Congress Catalog Number: 2019951337

Printed in Canada by Marquis Book Printing
10 9 8 7 6 5 4 3 2

Acquisitions editor: Bridget Thoreson
Managing editor: Claire Chun
Editor: Renee Rutledge
Proofreader: Kate St.Clair
Cover design: Justin Shirley
Interior design: what!design @ whatweb.com
Cover art: © Champ008/shutterstock.com
Interior art: page 64 © sailorlun/shutterstock.com
Layout: Jake Flaherty

IMPORTANT NOTE TO READERS: This book has been written and published for informational and educational purposes only. It is not intended to serve as medical advice or to be any form of medical treatment. You should always consult with your physician before altering or changing any aspect of your medical treatment. Do not stop or change any prescription medications without the guidance and advice of your physician. Any use of the information in this book is made on the reader's good judgment and is the reader's sole responsibility. This book is not intended to diagnose or treat any medical condition and is not a substitute for a physician. This book is independently authored and published and no sponsorship or endorsement of this book by, and no affiliation with, any trademarked brands or other products mentioned within is claimed or suggested. All trademarks that appear in this book belong to their respective owners and are used here for informational purposes only. The author and publisher encourage readers to patronize the quality brands mentioned in this book.

CONTENTS

INTRODUCTION

Welcome to the beginning of an exciting journey! As you work through this book, you will learn useful tools that will help you now and well into adulthood. The activities and prompts included are designed to help you understand the importance of knowing, accepting, and loving your true self. Self-love is a practical resource to help you balance your responsibilities, make healthy friendships, and strive to be the best version of yourself. By the time you reach the end of this workbook, you will know how to embed self-love into your day-to-day life.

Growing up, people have likely helped you by telling you what to do. Parents have given you bedtimes, teachers have given you deadlines, and so on. At this point in your life in particular, you are learning to take on the important task of monitoring yourself as you transition into adulthood. Consider this workbook a chance to practice self-reflection as you tune in to your personal gauge.

Please note that you are starting on a new, unfamiliar path. It is normal to be confused or even a bit scared. As you courageously take on this important path, you will encounter helpful vehicles to support your quest. On the other hand, it is possible that you may also find roadblocks that may temporarily hinder your journey.

Although challenging, this adventure is paved with the promise of growth, happiness, and love. Even the simple act of opening this book is a huge step in the right direction! You've chosen a personal pilgrimage to become a better version of yourself, and this dedication to discovering and loving your true self is incredibly powerful. As you work toward your personal goals, come back to this initial spark of motivation and be inspired! Although you may be focused on crossing the finish line, please remember that it is often the quest itself that makes the biggest impact.

Before you begin, take a moment to reflect. What caused you to start this workbook?

Although self-love is helpful for everyone at any age, the reasons we are drawn to self-love vary from person to person. For example, someone may recognize that they're struggling with standing up to toxic people and someone else might grow overwhelmed when thinking about choosing a future career. Though quite different, both are excellent reasons to invest in self-love.

As you begin your journey, you may even find that your reason may change, or you may accumulate multiple reasons that support your self-love venture. Reflecting on what brought you to open this workbook will be the first of many reflections that you will encounter in this process.

When a prompt arises, open your mind and heart. Take on the role of being your own good friend, not a toxic bully. Try your best not to judge your thoughts and feelings. Pay attention to what comes up as your immediate response, but be patient with yourself as well. The tasks in this workbook are not homework assignments with a prompt deadline. Allow yourself the time to fully explore the question at hand.

If you encounter a prompt that you've reflected on before, several thoughts may come to mind. On the other hand, you might also get stuck, especially if the prompt is new to you. It's perfectly okay to leave a question blank and return to it when the time feels right.

As you continue to explore, the concept of self-love will slowly become more clear to you. As a result, your reflections may become clearer with time. It may be helpful to return to previous segments to review what you have learned. Sometimes you may wish to add to your responses. You may even benefit from completing an activity more than once.

The following prompts will help you to reflect on why you are beginning a journey of self-love.

What has brought you to this path?

Why is learning about self-love important to you?

CHAPTER 1

SELF-LOVE

DEFINING SELF-LOVE

self-love \ *self-luhv* \ *n.* 1. The active practice of accepting, caring for, and encouraging oneself

Just as water and air are vital for survival, the need to love and be loved is important too. This includes your ability to honor, understand, and be kind to yourself.

Although the concept of self-love is not new, it has been gaining popularity in recent years. Many are realizing that love does not just exist between people, it exists within us as well. We need love from ourselves as much as, and sometimes more, than we do from others. On top of this, in our digital era, which exposes us to social comparisons, skewed views of reality, and cyberbullying earlier in life, self-love may be more critical for teens than ever before. Aside from the support you can get from the love of others, self-love empowers you to see and use your very own strength in order to lead a happier, healthier life.

Self-love begins with the task of being able to appreciate you for you. It is crucial to be kind and considerate toward yourself; however, self-love is more than a sentiment. In addition to your ability to give yourself care and encouragement, you must remember that self-love is an intentional practice.

Self-love is wondrously empowering, but contrary to popular belief, it is not always easy. It is more than sinking into a candlelit bubble bath, indulging in a delicious cupcake, or escaping to an island paradise. It is helpful to recognize that without darkness there cannot be an appreciation for light. That is why sincere self-love also acknowledges your weaknesses, faults, and obstacles. In the practice of self-love, you celebrate strengths and welcome opportunities for personal growth. Self-love provides you with the opportunity to see yourself completely: to value your triumphs and challenges. Self-love is a courageous practice. It requires the willingness to reflect on where you are, the bravery to consider where you want to be, and the tenacity to strive to be a better version of your true self.

This journey is ultimately an independent one. Although it is helpful to unite with others who are on a similar path, at the end of the day, self-growth is based on personal effort. The process of loving yourself is a subjective experience. Just because a tip has worked for many does not mean it will work for all. Respect your individuality as you attempt to follow the guidance provided in this book.

The process of self-love is not a summit to conquer. In reality, self-love is a continuous practice of caring for yourself. It takes dedication. It is not a choice that you make once, but a continuous decision to prioritize your wellness. Overall, self-love is an all-encompassing practice of recognizing your self-worth, being kind to yourself, and fostering your self-growth throughout the course of your life.

Just as the journey of self-love differs from person to person, the definition may vary as well. In the space below, share what self-love means to you.

THE IMPORTANCE OF SELF-LOVE

Claudia has loved playing soccer since she was a little girl. She met most of her best friends playing soccer throughout the years and has become a key player in her varsity team. A few months ago, Claudia started dating James. She has been missing many of her practices to be with him and this has caused a strain on her friendships. Today, she talked to James to share that soccer is important to her and that she can't keep missing soccer to spend time with him. James was offended and broke up with her. Claudia is devastated and can't bear to play soccer this afternoon.

Sameer has just transferred to a new school. In his old neighborhood he spent a lot of time with his extended family and never felt lonely or excluded. Sameer feels like an outsider at his school, and on top of this, he's been getting bullied a lot. Recently, Sameer started getting mean messages and harassed on his social media. For the first time, Sameer is not enjoying going to school. He is constantly distracted in his classes and his grades are starting to drop. Sameer is ashamed to share about how this hurts him, and he hasn't told anyone.

Lanisha has always been a well-rounded student and is on the path to becoming valedictorian. She dreams of becoming a surgeon, just like her parents. Lanisha is starting to question if she is prepared enough for college. Her distracting thoughts have made it hard to complete her scholarship applications on top of her usual work. Lanisha is finding it difficult to balance but is embarrassed to ask for help. Desperate, she stole her friend's ADHD medication and has been using it to stay on top of her responsibilities.

Now that you have a definition of self-love, consider how self-love applies to Claudia, Sameer, and Lanisha.

What examples of self-love do you see within Claudia?

What examples of self-love do you see within Sameer?

What examples of self-love do you see within Lanisha?

How do you think Claudia's life may change if she improved her self-love?

How do you think Sameer's life may change if he improved his self-love?

How do you think Lanisha's life may change if she improved her self-love?

Claudia, Sameer, and Lanisha are average people not too different from you. Like anyone else, they need self-love. From these short cases we get a peek into a time in their lives when they are lacking self-love. At this point in time, Claudia, Sameer, and Lanisha are all struggling to honor their worth. Each of them does not realize the importance of caring for themselves.

Each of them has disconnected from their true selves and has been facing consequences as a result of that severance. Excited about her new relationship, Claudia was invested in love, but forgot her self-love in the process. Sameer's troubled self-esteem and self-respect are beginning to take a toll on his wellness, and he is becoming isolated in the process. On the outside, someone may not guess that Lanisha is struggling; however, her perfectionism is causing her to make poor decisions to try to prove her worth.

Like anyone else, Claudia, Sameer, and Lanisha are all capable of making the choice to focus on self-love. At this point in their lives, the brave choice to explore and reconnect with their genuine selves can help them to improve their lives. They can discover the strengths that they have but may have been ignoring. They can understand their areas for growth and explore them with patience and kindness. As they choose a self-loving lifestyle they will be able to care for and respect not only themselves, but others well.

Without a strong sense of love for yourself, you may experience the following feelings. Shade in the boxes that you experience.

Anxiety	Hopelessness	Sadness
Carelessness	Insecurity	Shame
Criminal behavior	Materialism	Stagnancy
Defensiveness	Negligence	Suicidal thoughts
Depression	Prejudice	Unhealthy coping

On the other hand, with a strong sense of love for yourself you may benefit from gains in the following areas. Shade in the things you would like to have. As you continue to work on this book, notice how your experience of these benefits may start to increase.

Academic achievement	Empowerment	Motivation
Altruism	Encouragement	Passion
Belonging	Enthusiasm	Relationship quality
Career success	Happiness	Self-care
Confidence	Inspiration	Social support
Coping	Love	Physical health

SELF-LOVE FOR TEENAGERS

We need self-love throughout our lives. As you transition from childhood into adulthood, you experience several changes that make self-love more possible than ever before. Teenage years are actually a pivotal time to foster self-love. The earlier you establish your self-love practice, the sooner you can reap the benefits. As a continuous process, self-love can become second nature if you start early and prioritize your practice in the years to come.

IMPROVED THINKING Your brain matures in your teenage years, allowing you to process information more deeply. For example, while you may not be learning more letters in the alphabet, you can now combine letters to form words and sentences in a way you would not have been able to in the past. With this expanded thinking comes the ability to contemplate and comprehend abstract concepts. In the past you may have seen necessities for survival as literal (e.g., food, water). Now you are able to realize that some things that may be hard to see, describe, or quantify could be just as important (e.g., self-love). As a teenager you are also able to consider views that differ from your own. This allows you to generate multiple perspectives and helps with interpersonal relations.

RESPONSE INHIBITION As a teenager, you tend to focus on the short-term. Although you are now able to see long-term repercussions, the teen brain tends to waver toward immediate gratification. Substances like marijuana and alcohol can further lower the threshold for inhibitions. While changes in the brain make your response inhibition particularly weak, knowing this can empower you to take a step back and slow down when making decisions.

ORGANIZATION AND PLANNING While in-the-moment decisions may be a weakness in adolescence, improved organizational and planning skills make long-term thinking possible. Self-love requires the ability to think not just for the present moment, but to understand the consequences that may last far beyond the present. Developmental improvements help you make adequate preparations, deeply reflect on a thorough plan, and invest in your self-growth. For example, these improvements allow you to recognize that instead of waiting until the day before to cram for your chemistry final, you can take the time to study weeks in advance. Doing this allows you to recognize where you need extra help.

EMOTIONAL REGULATION Your brain has developed to provide you with the ability to think about your emotions. To date, you have been able to experience emotions, but you may not have been able to reflect on them as clearly as you can now. Now, if you choose, you can reflect on your emotions. From this, you may better understand and manage your emotions as well. For example, imagine your best friend says something to offend you. In the past you may have responded impulsively on your negative feelings. However, now you have the ability to pause, contemplate the situation, and carefully select a response. The changes in your brain allow you to connect your thoughts, feelings, and behaviors. These connections are helpful in developing your overall emotional and social intelligence.

IDENTITY DEVELOPMENT As a teenager you continue to develop your sense of self. While you explore your environment and learn about others around you, you begin to discern who you are. Adolescence is a key time to develop self-awareness and to differentiate how you may be similar to and different from others. At this developmental stage you begin to make sense of how you fit in the world. Since self-love is subjective, this knowledge is crucial as it helps you know what is right for you rather than focus on what works for others.

WHAT SELF-LOVE ISN'T

Self-love is often mistaken for something it is not. This misinformation causes people to ignore the importance of self-love and face the consequences noted on the table on page 8. To clear that up, let's be specific about what self-love is not.

ENTITLEMENT When a person has a sense of entitlement, they may believe they are unconditionally owed something regardless of their efforts, merit, or context. For example, Steve recently passed his driving test. Not only does he believe that he will be returning home to a brand-new car, but he believes he deserves a luxury car similar to the cars his parents drive. Steve is convinced he deserves an extra-special car just because.

Entitlement should not be confused with the idea of recognizing your worth. One could argue that compassion, care, and acceptance are as fundamental as water, food, or shelter. Therefore, self-worth may also be essential. When taken out of proportion and context, this may look like entitlement. Self-love isn't about why you deserve a billion dollars, a fancy yacht, or a mansion. It isn't an overtly ambitious jump. On the other hand, it isn't elite or exclusive, but a core aspect of humanity.

SELFISHNESS Self-love requires that you shift some of your attention to yourself in order to be self-aware. However, there's quite a difference between self-obsession and self-love. Being aware of your own needs does not solely benefit yourself, but those around you as well.

In order to care for others, you have to care for yourself first. Prior to taking off on an airplane, the flight attendant instructs fliers that in the case of an emergency, regardless of who is nearby, it's critical to first place on your oxygen mask before helping others. We wouldn't dare tell someone who abides by this regulation that they are truly selfish. A self-focus is not egocentric; ultimately, a self-focus helps you and others.

SINFUL A sin is an act that is not only inappropriate, but often violent. Self-love is just the opposite. Self-love isn't meant to go against a principle or moral grounding; it's an enlightened journey to care for yourself and others. Investing in your self-love prompts a domino effect of care and compassion for those around you.

Some people may view self-love as a practice that goes against their values and beliefs. Just as everyone is unique, their interpretation of scripture may vary as well. If you are struggling with differentiating self-love from sin, it may be helpful for you to research and reflect on whether or not a conflict truly exists.

It may also be worthwhile to consider the commonalities in various world religions. A common theme in religious doctrines involves being a moral person. Associated traits such as benevolence, forgiveness, and personal growth all align well with the practice of self-love.

More specifically, the golden rule of treating others as you want to be treated is the essence of self-love. This phrase reminds us to treat others kindly. We should also remember that this includes treating ourselves with kindness as well.

AN EXCUSE Self-love is an engaging process that comes with many positive benefits. With that being said, the journey is not always an easy one. In the practice of self-love, it's important to be able to recognize your needs and take steps to fulfill them. This may include mental health days, binge-watching your favorite series, and indulging in your favorite home-cooked meal—but it is certainly not to be confused with an exploitation of all things good.

The full process of self-love includes the good and the bad. In reality, overdoing certain self-care skills could actually be neglectful as you avoid the difficult but necessary aspects of personal growth. Self-love can be a challenging process that warrants courage every step of the way.

First, you must be willing to recognize your areas for growth. Then, you create a potentially challenging but necessary plan to fill that gap. Finally, you pursue your goal with dedication. Considering these challenging steps, self-love is not an excuse but hard work.

It is your responsibility to know the difference between sincere self-love and your hall pass to escape the world. You can pursue true self-love by taking accountability and responsibility as you courageously embark on arduous paths.

"Love yourself first and everything else falls into line. You really have to love yourself to get anything done in this world."

—Lucille Ball

OBSTACLES IN SELF-LOVE

"Your task is not to seek for love, but merely to seek and find all the barriers within yourself that you have built against it."

—Rumi

As you prepare for your journey in self-love, it can be helpful to be aware of what may be holding you back from pursuing this path. Knowing what is standing in the way of you living a happier, healthier life can better prepare you to tackle these challenges. Please remember that self-love begins with "self." While we all need self-love, this journey is specific to you. You will not face the same obstacles as someone you know. Although everyone is different, there are some common concerns that may stand in the way of you loving yourself.

ABUSE Abuse is cruel and violent treatment of another person. Common forms of abuse include physical, sexual, and psychological. Although all forms of abuse may have psychological consequences, since psychological abuse includes pain without obvious physical harm, concerns tend to be further ignored, minimized, or difficult to recognize. Sticks, stones, and words can be painful. Name-calling, yelling, insulting, threatening, excluding, mocking, humiliating, and criticizing all have the potential to be deeply painful and powerful offenses that often prohibit a person's ability to love themselves.

All types of abuse have the potential to cause severe impairment. Even memories of abuse can trigger individuals to experience consequences in the present moment. When an individual experiences triggers, they may become distracted from their self-love practice.

Abuse may happen at the hands of someone who is known and trusted. This person could be a loved one, such as a parent or friend. This betrayal can cause a lack of trust in oneself and in others. It can also prompt issues with self-esteem, self-confidence, and self-respect.

It can be difficult to discuss abuse. As a consequence, some individuals hold onto the secret of their abuse. Holding onto this secret does not keep them safe from feelings of shame and guilt. Without the safety to discuss these feelings and experiences, they cannot experience healing. Without the ability to seek help, they may have to face the consequences alone, and even worse, the abuse may continue.

COMPARISONS A common way you might harm yourself without even realizing it is by comparing yourself to others. It may begin as a simple observation, and sometimes your comparisons can be motivational. For example, you may notice that a studious friend continues to earn higher grades. You might admire your friend and make the connection that the grades are related to effort. This comparison may give you the motivation to invest more time in your studies.

However, comparisons are not always as innocent. Comparisons have the potential to transform into negative self-statements, and when this happens, they may form large roadblocks in your journey of self-love. It is one thing to utilize a comparison to help you assess your progress, but when exploited, a useful tactic becomes fuel for your inner critic. The example above could take a turn for the worse if you were to become obsessed with checking grades and begin to attach your worth to earning a higher grade than your friend. When this comparison gets out of control you might even neglect other things that are important to you, such as sleep, and your competitiveness may even cost you your friendship.

Comparisons are especially concerning when they are habitual, obsessive, and/or constant. As negative self-talk increases and loudens, it can be difficult to make room for positivity. Over time, what may have been a seemingly simple comparison could create an unrealistic, impossible standard for yourself. These thoughts create a mentality that inhibits the acceptance and kindness necessary for self-love.

MENTAL ILLNESS Mental health and self-love are connected. When you love yourself, you are able to foster your mental wellness. Self-love can certainly be helpful for those who live with mental health diagnoses, especially those pertaining to anxiety, depression, interpersonal problems, and trauma. On the other hand, if you are struggling with a mental health concern, you may become distracted from your self-love journey.

Tending to proper mental health care is fundamental to a successful journey of self-love. While everyone can benefit from self-love in their lives, loving oneself is not the solution to mental illness. This workbook can be a helpful resource in your mental health; however, it does not substitute for mental health treatment.

Furthermore, consistent setbacks on the path of self-love may point to an unattended mental health concern. If this occurs, it is important to consult with a mental health professional to assist you in bringing previously unidentified concerns to light. Raising this awareness may be an empowering shift in your process. When you have the will to grow, the appropriate mental health resources can help you transition from mental illness to mental wellness.

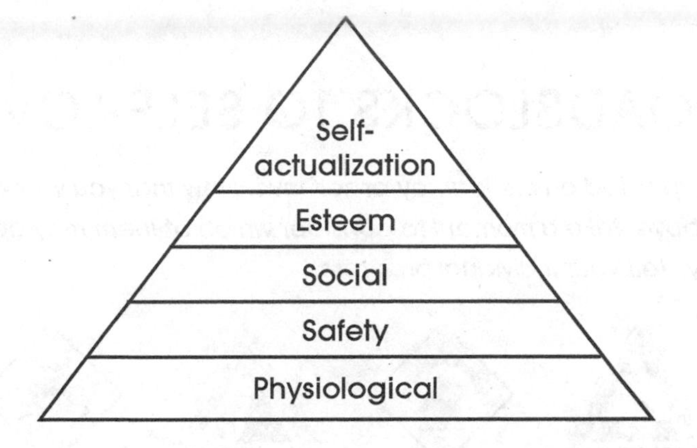

Maslow's hierarchy of needs

DANGER Existential psychologist Abraham Maslow asserted that humans have five basic needs: physiological, safety, social, esteem, and self-actualization. According to the hierarchy our needs are sequential. Like a staircase, lower-level needs are required to ascend to higher levels. Maslow believed that humans aspire to have all of these needs met and experience a sense of genuine fulfillment when this is achieved.

To achieve improvements in self-esteem, self-growth, and self-love you must first establish foundational needs—physiological, safety, and social. This reminds us that while self-love may be a personal goal, we have to prioritize other needs to create the ability to meet our self-love needs. An unwillingness to consider a hierarchy could cause you to become frustrated by placing your energy on self-love when it is not presently possible. You wouldn't enroll in calculus without rudimentary mathematic knowledge, and you should approach your needs similarly.

For individuals who are struggling to put food on the table or even find shelter (physiological and safety needs), the ability to focus on self-love is not unneeded, it may simply be a luxury within that context. If a challenging phase in life shakes your foundation, temporarily abandoning your current self-love path to regain your equilibrium is certainly justified. Take the time to create a solid foundation and when the time is right, revisit your self-love path.

In reference to the social domain, we need others just as they may need us. Self-love is not a selfish journey. Pursing a goal of improved self-love does not mean that you have to ignore the needs of those who are important to you. When our loved ones need your attention, care, and love, it is understandable to take a detour from your journey to help them.

Our esteem is made up of how we view ourselves and how others view us as well. While we may often rely on others to serve as a mirror for our esteem, it is important to remember that self-esteem is fostered internally. Therefore, fulfilling our esteem needs means maintaining a balance of our views and those of others. Regardless of the level, our needs may be tested throughout our lives, and it is helpful to remember to first fulfill our essential needs to allow us to continue on our self-love journey.

ROADBLOCKS TO SELF-LOVE

Roadblocks are to be expected on the journey of self-love. Now that you've explored the common obstacles mentioned above, take a moment to consider which of them may apply as well as the unique hurdles that may stall your individual progress.

____

____

____

____

____

PREPARING FOR YOUR JOURNEY

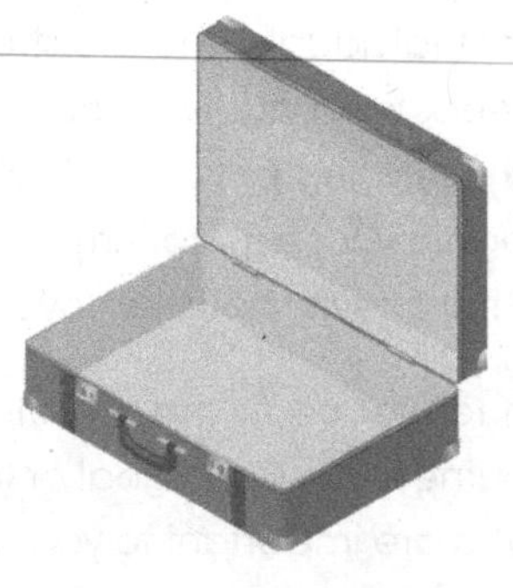

This workbook will likely be easy to read, but harder to practice. Unfortunately, simply reading the material will not improve your self-love. You can skim through the pages of this workbook quite quickly, but processing and applying the core concepts will take more time.

This journey will require patience. If you were preparing for a marathon, you wouldn't expect yourself to run 26.2 miles on the first day of training. Chances are that you would not view this as a defeat. Instead, you'd intentionally condition yourself for the challenge by allocating the necessary time, energy, and preparations. Furthermore, you'd be kind and encouraging to yourself as you strove to reach your goal.

To fully engage in this journey, you need to be open and honest with yourself. There will certainly be peaks in which you will recognize your growth, and valleys consisting of difficult moments in which you may feel vulnerable or even uncomfortable. When this happens, you may be tempted to shut the book and abandon your journey. While knowing your limit is an excellent practice in self-love, making a habit of veering around essential points in the process may inhibit your growth.

Allow yourself to take a break. When you are ready to reopen the book, you might find it helpful to revisit a previously finished activity that you enjoyed or a prompt that was similar to the one you found yourself stuck on. Another option is to skip over the difficult task and return to it when you have improved your self-love in other ways and are prepared to take on that activity.

While self-love is an individualized journey, you do not need to embark on it alone. Social support can be a helpful way to navigate the different dimensions of self-love. If a loved one is also willing to foster self-love, it may be helpful to join forces to create mutual support. Use your time together to discuss the concepts and perhaps even share how you responded to the activities. Be sure to still allow time for your personal reflection. Be mindful that while you are united in your quest to improve your self-love, your experiences may vary. Welcome your differences in perspectives as an opportunity to learn about the broader scope of self-love.

When you meet the end of this workbook, it does not mean that your self-love journey is complete. Your unique, reflective, and engaging journey to improve your overall practice of self-love will persist beyond this workbook because true self-love is a continuous process rather than a destination. You may find it helpful to complete an activity more than one time, and to revisit the workbook at different phases in your life. If you choose to do this, it can be helpful to complete the activities on scrap paper. Date each page, fold it, and store it at that page in the book. This will not only allow you to return to the activity, but observe how your answers may change or remain the same over time.

What do you need to prepare, prior to embarking on this journey?

____

____

____

____

____

SEVEN SEGMENTS OF SELF-LOVE

The remaining chapters of the book each cover one of the seven segments of self-love. Before you begin to explore each area deeply, take a moment to consider where you believe you are in each area at this moment in time:

1. Self-awareness is the ability to recognize who you are, how you influence the world, and how the world influences you. When you are self-aware, you are in tune with your thoughts, feelings, and behaviors. This self-awareness then permits you to step into your power as you begin to take charge of your life.

2. Self-exploration is encapsulated by the willingness to delve into learning about yourself. Once you hone your self-awareness, self-exploration becomes an option. Self-exploration is the deeper level of courageously improving your self-knowledge in an effort to be a better person.

3. Self-care consists of a wide variety of tasks that you require to take care of your overall wellness. While the specific methods of tending to your needs may vary from person to person, everyone needs self-care in order to maintain a sense of balance.

4. Self-esteem is how you view your overall self. It may be influenced by others, but ultimately, it is your perception of how you recognize and value your self-worth.

5. Self-kindness is the skill of being friendly to yourself. When you are kind to someone else that person may feel validated and supported. You can benefit from giving that same kindness to yourself as well.

6. Self-respect is the empowered ability to advocate for yourself. When you have a healthy sense of self-respect, you are able to recognize and assert boundaries with yourself and others.

7. Self-growth is the continual process of seeking opportunities to learn, love, and thrive. Self-love is an ongoing journey in which you acknowledge that there is always room for growth; and hence, the opportunity to learn and grow is always present.

Based on your reflection, shade in each petal to help you recognize which areas are strong and which areas may need improvement.

CHAPTER 2

SELF-AWARENESS

Self-awareness begins with your openness to look within yourself. Through introspection, you can better understand your thoughts, feelings, desires, motives, and overall self. Think of yourself as an observer in your journey. As you focus your attention on your process, you will be less affected by self-judgment and criticism along the way.

With self-awareness, you can be a conscientious and engaged advocate for your well-being. Allowing yourself to reflect helps you to recognize when you need self-love and allows you to act promptly on fulfilling those gaps. Without this recognition you could find yourself lost on your self-love journey.

One way to help improve your self-awareness is through journaling. Journaling is a helpful tool for tuning into your awareness, connecting you to your inner world, and reflecting at any stage in your self-love journey. Writing will be encouraged throughout this book as a way for you to recognize your views and reactions on a deeper level.

Some of the activities will be open-ended and will ask you to reflect on a broad topic. Other times journaling can follow a specific prompt.

Let's try an open-ended reflection on your self-awareness.

Explore your thoughts, feelings, and desires in this very moment.

ALL MY FEELS

"Be who you are and say what you feel, because those who mind don't matter and those who matter don't mind."

—Dr. Seuss

Emotional awareness is a key aspect of self-awareness. It is helpful to be able to recognize how you are feeling in any given moment. Attuning awareness can help you foster your self-love. For example, if you can pinpoint when you feel overwhelmed while studying for an exam, you can be empowered to tend to your self-care with a walk around the block.

100 Feeling Words

Agitated
Alert
Alienated
Amazed
Angry
Annoyed
Apathetic
Appalled
Appreciated
Apprehensive
Astonished
Awed
Betrayed
Bored
Calm
Caring
Chipper
Committed
Compassionate
Concerned
Confident
Confused
Content
Creative
Curious
Dedicated
Defensive
Dejected
Disappointed
Disgusted
Eager
Embarrassed
Encouraged
Enraged
Enthusiastic
Excited
Fearful
Focused
Fortunate
Frustrated
Furious
Grateful
Happy
Heartbroken
Honored
Hopeful
Hopeless
Horrified
Humiliated
Inadequate
Independent
Inferior
Infuriated
Insecure
Inspired
Intrigued
Irate
Irritated
Joyful
Listless
Lonely
Loving
Mad
Miserable
Motivated
Neglected
Nervous
Offended
Optimistic
Ostracized
Passive
Peaceful
Perplexed
Playful
Powerful
Productive
Proud
Rejected
Remorseful
Resentful

Sad	Shocked	Threatened	Vigilant
Safe	Stressed	Tired	Vulnerable
Scared	Submissive	Trustful	Weak
Sensitive	Sullen	Uninterested	Withdrawn
Serene	Thoughtful	Unworthy	Worried

EMOTIONAL AWARENESS

Take a moment to tune into your emotions. In this very instance, how do you feel?

In this moment I feel...

____

____

____

____

____

Delve deeper—are you aware of why you feel the way you do?

For example: *I feel excited because I am learning how to improve my self-love.*

I feel ______________________________ because ______________

____

I feel ______________________________ because ______________

____

I feel ______________________________ because ______________

____

EMOTIONAL EQUATIONS

When reflecting on your feelings, you may notice a combination of emotions in a given situation. This is common to experience. Recognizing that you are likely to have more than one feeling at a time helps you to broaden your awareness in a given situation. Reflect on how you feel with the following combinations of emotions:

Relaxed + Creative =

When I feel relaxed and creative I am able to think clearly. My best ideas come up when I'm in this zone.

Happy + Sad =

Excited + Confident =

Lonely + Insecure =

Inadequate + Foolish =

Playful + Cheerful =

Important + Thankful =

If you found it easy to think of times in which you experienced these combinations, that may be a sign of a strong emotional awareness. Continue to consider combinations of emotional equations to help you improve your self-awareness.

If it was difficult for you, that's okay. Be patient with yourself. Now that you understand that feelings can be complex from context to context, you will be able to practice refining your awareness in the present. Feel free to return to these reflections to continue to foster your emotional awareness.

EMOTIONAL INTELLIGENCE

Knowing what prompts your emotions is another self-awareness skill that helps you to better understand yourself and the world around you.

Let's explore your emotions a bit further. For each emotion below, consider how you are before and after the emotion. Use general examples that are common to you or specific memories from the past.

Example from Sam:

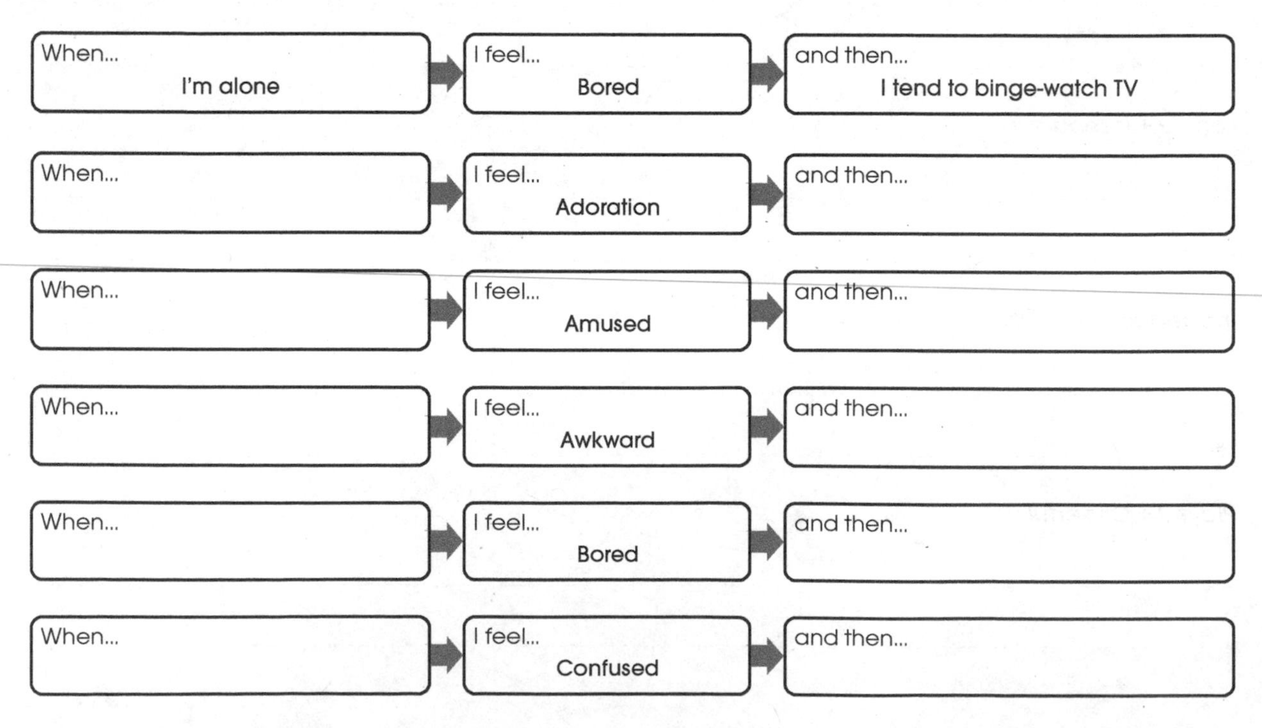

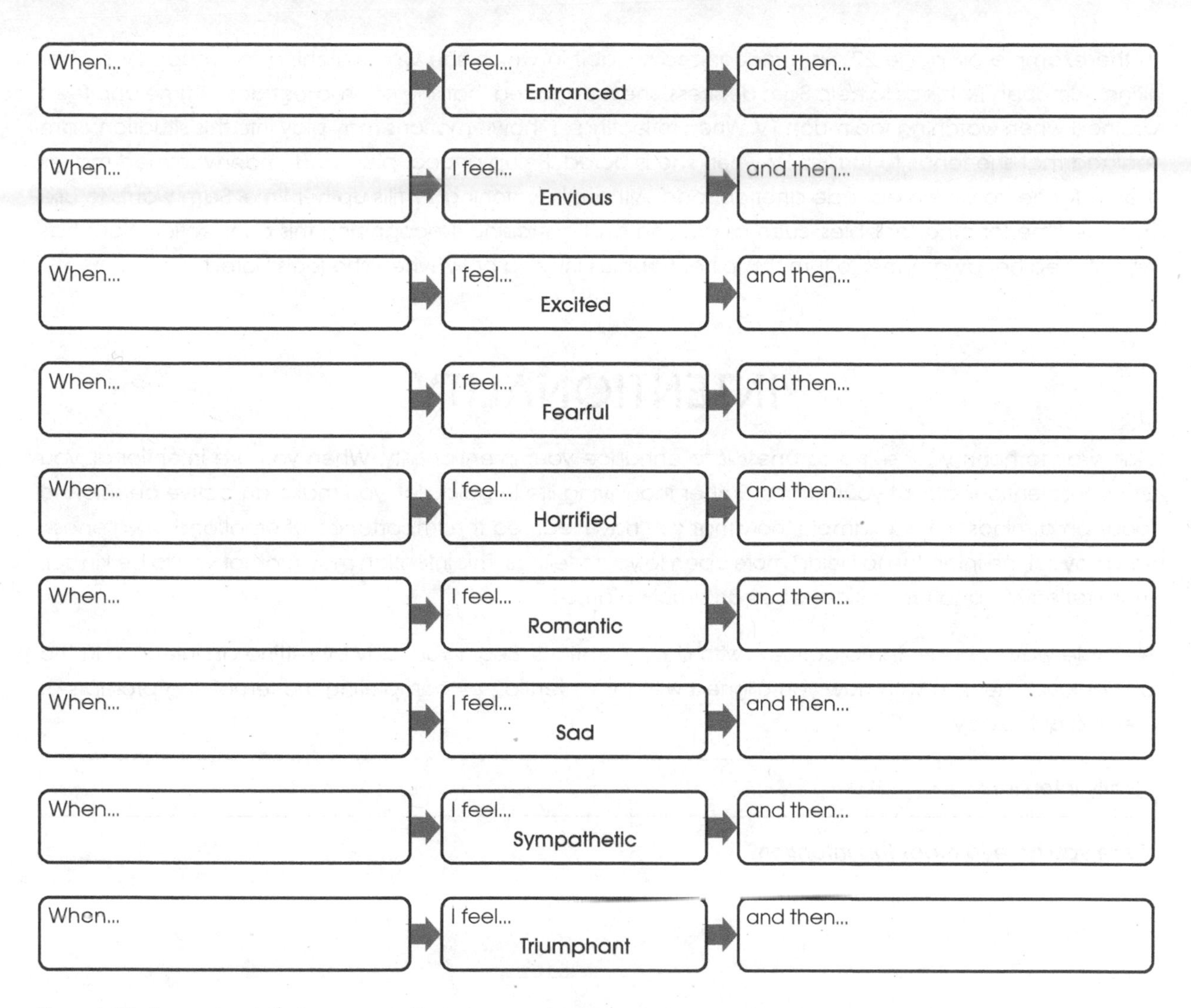

The ability to understand your emotions is a part of your emotional intelligence. Without this skill you may not be able to learn, grow, and heal from negative emotions. Knowing your state of being before you experience an emotion could help you understand it better and learn how to regulate that emotion.

In the exercise above, you were able to practice two aspects of understanding: the root and the effect. The root is what is underneath an emotion whereas the effect occurs as a result of the emotion arising. Oftentimes the root may include a specific trigger. Triggers and effects can be thoughts, feelings, or behaviors. They can include people or things as well.

Exploring your emotional roots and affects allows you to consider the depth of your emotional experience. When you develop this skill you can begin to understand how your feelings may affect your thoughts and behaviors. On top of this, improving your awareness of your emotional state can help you to know when you are struggling and may need help.

In the example on page 22, Sam recognized a habit in which she was watching too much TV for her liking. Although TV tends to help Sam de-stress, she recognized that she often loses track of time and feels drained when watching too much TV. When reflecting on how emotions may play into this situation, Sam realized that she tends to turn to TV when she is bored. Being unoccupied and underwhelmed makes it easy for her to watch episode after episode. Although watching TV fills up her time, Sam wants to use her free time for other hobbies, such as crafting and exercising. Recognizing this connection, Sam has heightened her awareness to turn first to her hobbies instead of TV when she feels bored.

INTENTIONALITY

One way to hone your self-awareness is to enhance your intentionality. When you are intentional, you are conscientious about your efforts. Rather than living life in autopilot, you make an active decision to focus on a mindset. For example, now that you have learned the importance of emotional awareness, you may set the intention to being more open to your feelings. This intention may prompt you to be kinder, more reflective, and less critical when an emotion arises.

A simple way to begin this practice is with daily intentions. Begin your day by setting an intention in the box below. Check in with how you aligned with that intention by completing the remaining prompts at the end of the day.

Daily intention:

Were you able to meet this intention?

____

____

Did you encounter any obstacles in meeting this intention?

____

____

What self-loving intention would you like to set for tomorrow?

____

____

MINDFULNESS

In our world it is easy to be distracted and often difficult to be present or tune in to ourselves. This can block our self-awareness. The practice of mindfulness can be a helpful tool to overcome this common hurdle.

The benefits of mindful practice include improvements in memory, sense of self, empathy, coping, and decision making, and reductions in worries, stress, and perceptions of chronic pain. Although mindfulness may seem simple, small adjustments have been shown to make a substantial impact. Mindfulness methods have been powerful enough to reduce symptoms of post-traumatic stress disorder in veterans and symptoms of distress in cancer patients.

Mindfulness dates back thousands of years to ancient Asia. The practice has spread across the globe and evolved over time. Today, the meaning of mindfulness may be interpreted differently from person to person. For the context of this workbook, think of mindfulness as a sincere state of presence in which you are conscientious, attentive, and engaged. When you are mindful, you are not consumed by what has happened or what is to come. Instead, you are actively involved in the here and now. Additionally, you are a calm and kind observer who is immersed in the current experience and is not overwhelmed by judgments.

Mindfulness does not fit into the stereotype of seated and stationary meditation. Hence, you can practice mindfulness when talking, eating, and walking. When you are mindful, you are engaged and nonjudgmentally observant in the present moment. To be mindful, you are a self-aware observer in your own life. If you attune your awareness in a given moment and rid yourself of criticism, you are practicing the essence of mindfulness.

Here are three ways to use mindfulness to hone your self-awareness. These three activities will help you to train your mindfulness muscle. They may seem simple, but the practices may be quite difficult. Use them as a challenge to continue to strengthen your mindfulness muscle. Remember to be patient with yourself.

BREATHING: As you read this, bring your attention to your breathing. Can you hear your breathing? Recognize where the breath enters the body. Note where the breath leaves the body. Does the air meet the top of the lungs? Do your lungs fill to capacity? Does your chest rise, or your stomach contract?

Begin to slow your breath. As you continue, notice how this change in pace affects your body. Pay attention to the subtle movement that each breath brings to the body, with every inhale and every exhale. Now, place one hand on your chest as you continue to breathe. Notice the sensation of the lungs filling with air and decompressing with each exhale.

Inhale as you slowly count 1-2-3. Take a moment to pause. Release the breath as you reverse the count 3-2-1. Take another pause. Repeat this pattern. You may wish to elongate your breath, adding counts for your inhale, exhale, or pauses. Continue this pattern as needed.

BODY SCAN: Find a comfortable seated position. Soften your gaze, this may simply be lowered eyelids or you may choose to close your eyes altogether. Bring your attention to your body. Check your posture. Notice how your body is grounded. Now, bring your awareness to your breath. Slowly inhale and slowly exhale. Begin to elongate your exhales, making them longer than your inhales.

Continue to breathe as you bring your awareness to your feet. Notice any tension that you may have in the bottoms of your feet, your ankles, or toes. Take a deep inhale, and on a slow exhale try to relax your feet.

Continue to breathe as you bring your awareness to your knees. Notice any tension that you may have in your knees, shins, or calves. Take a deep inhale, and with your next exhale try to release this tension.

Moving up the legs, notice any tension that you may be holding in your thighs, pelvis, or glutes. Inhale, and release this tension as you exhale. Bring your attention up to your midsection, then up to your chest. As you inhale note any tension in these areas and release with your elongated exhale.

Bring your awareness to your shoulders through the tips of your fingers. Recognize the tension that may be in your arms with your inhale, and release that tension with your exhale.

Finally, notice any tension from your neck to the crown of your head. Take the longest inhale of this practice, and release any tension from the crown of your head to the base of your feet with the longest exhale of this practice. Using this elongated breath, on the next inhale squeeze every inch of your body tight. Curl the toes, create fists, squeeze your glutes, and tighten your face. On the next elongated exhale, release this tremendous tension, allowing your body to sink and relax. Continue to breathe as needed.

CLOUD WATCHING: Mental noise can distract us from being mindful and self-aware. One thought often leads to another thought. This activity can help you to streamline, and perhaps even quiet your thoughts. Through this practice you are able to acknowledge your thoughts and allow yourself to release them. Your focus can shift from questioning or avoiding your thoughts to observing them.

Imagine that you are lying in a lush green field, looking up at the clouds. As they move across the sky, you observe them and let them pass. Imagine each of your thoughts is attached to a single cloud. Recognize each thought as it enters your scope and allow it to pass with the subtle rotation of the Earth.

From time to time you may experience a storm cloud. These clouds include thoughts that inhibit your presence, engagement, and nonjudgmental mindset. These thoughts are difficult to release. Examples may be upcoming tasks, worries about another person, or even random distractions. A key in self-awareness is recognizing when these clouds arise. It is senseless to try to fight a storm, but we can still be aware of when a storm is coming and its cause.

SELF-KNOWLEDGE

"We don't see things as they are, we see them as we are."

—Anais Nin

When you improve your personal awareness, you begin to learn more about yourself. You can practice honing your self-awareness in short moments, such as choosing what to eat for lunch, but can also recognize deeper and consistent pieces of who you are, such as your hopes for the future. From this type of reflection you may be able to improve your self-knowledge. Knowing yourself is essential to understand what self-love means specifically to you. In addition to learning more about yourself, it helps you to differentiate from others, and learn more about them as well. Say, for example, you are chatting with your friends about your favorite movies. You may find that the movies you enjoy sometimes overlap, and those may be representative of who you are as people. On the other hand, having distinct favorites could also provide some insight into how you are different. Connecting to self-knowledge can allow you to go deeper than preferences. Fostering your self-knowledge allows you to consider what helps or stands in the way of your self-love. When you connect to your self-knowledge, you can see strengths and capabilities you may not have previously recognized.

Use the categories below to delve into what you know about you.

I am	I have	I love

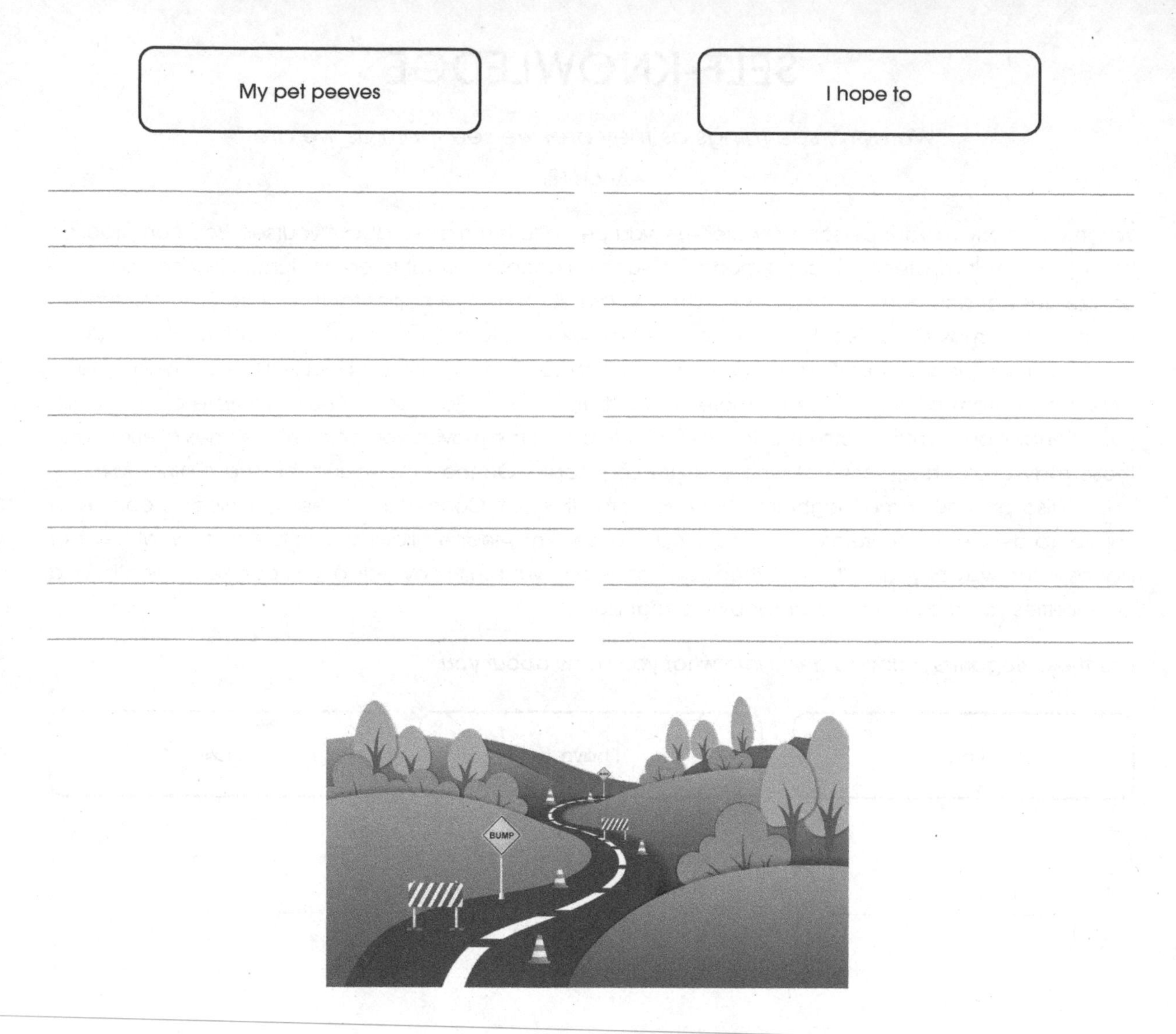

HIGHLIGHTING STRENGTHS

When you prepared for your self-love journey you considered the roadblocks that you may face along the way (see Roadblocks to Self-Love on page 14). While practicing self-love, you will learn that your strengths can help you to endure difficult moments. If you take the time to become aware of your strengths, then you will be able to use them in a time of need.

What provides you with the momentum to propel forward on your self-love path?

Example: *My perseverance helps me to come back to my goals even if I experience a setback.*

FINDING BLIND SPOTS

"Sometimes you can't see yourself clearly until you see yourself through the eyes of others."

—Ellen DeGeneres

Everyone has blind spots. Even if you are sincerely dedicated to your self-love journey, you will still have blind spots. Sometimes others can see your blind spot while your own view may be blocked. Expanding your perspective can help you to get a peek of your blind spots.

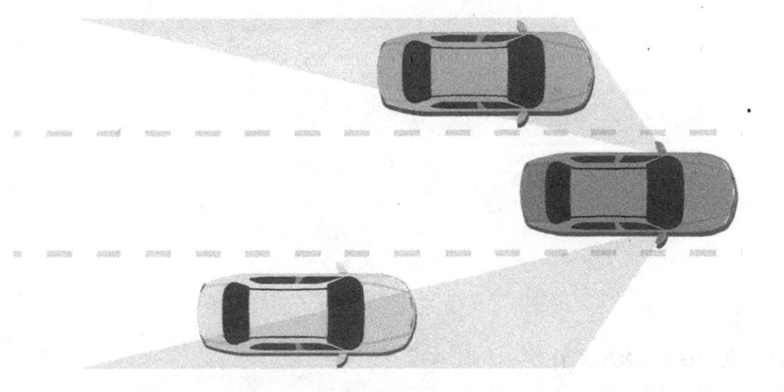

A surface level example is when someone informs you that you have food stuck in your teeth that you didn't realize was there from hours prior. A deeper example would be if you perceive yourself to be a certain way, while others may not. Imagine you are working on a group project. You notice that your team members are talking over one another with their differing opinions, and two individuals are clearly vying for the role of the leader. In recognizing this you become overwhelmed and choose to keep quiet to avoid adding fuel to the fire. A week later one of your teammates accuses you of being a hands-off team member and not contributing to the project.

FEEDBACK

Can you think of a time when you provided feedback to help someone learn what was in their blind spot? Reflecting on what helped and hindered this process can help you plan for the future.

Feedback is information provided to encourage improvement. When given from a trusted source, such as a good friend or positive mentor, feedback can help you to see what may exist in your blind spots. Genuine feedback is constructive, caring, and motivated by the intent to foster growth.

Can you think of a time when someone may have tried to provide you with feedback to illuminate something in your blind spot?

Were you open to this feedback?

How can you be open to feedback in the future?

Being open to feedback in your journey can help you to grow. As you develop your own view, you can still benefit from the perspectives of others. On the other hand, there may also be times that you may choose to respectfully set feedback aside. As a continuous process, feedback can be useful in refining your growth process.

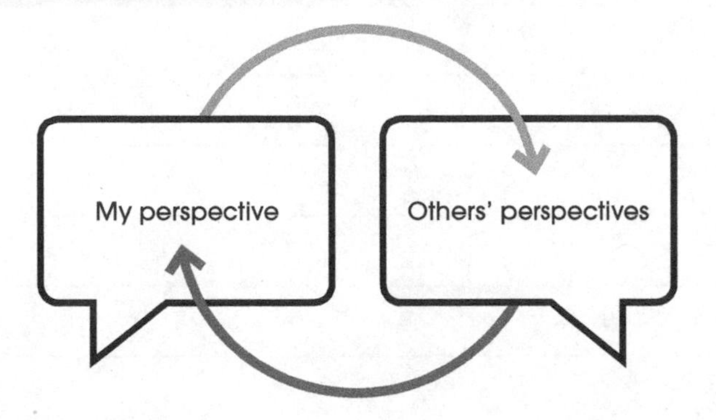

Imagine you are learning to play the guitar for the first time. Your music teacher gives you feedback to help you tweak your skills and enhance your abilities. After using the constructive notes you notice that your skills have improved and you feel a boost in confidence. Your instructor also notices your progression and provides you with feedback to challenge your new level of skill. In this process, the feedback is not because you are a terrible player. The feedback is both a reward for hard work and an opportunity to continue to prosper.

SELF-AWARENESS CHAPTER REFLECTION

CHAPTER 3

SELF-EXPLORATION

Self-exploration is the courage to learn about yourself in order to improve your knowledge of who you are. You can gain self-knowledge with self-awareness, then deepen it with self-exploration.

The path of self-exploration may include twists and turns. Choosing self-exploration shows that you are brave because this is not always an easy process. For example, at the moment you may not know your hopes and dreams for the future. This may be because you are focusing on the present, and trying to take life one day at a time. On the other hand, it could also be that you are avoiding thinking about the future because it feels scary and overwhelming. When you self-explore you may encounter these deeper fears.

There may be times that you are not ready or prepared to learn about yourself. However, a habit of disconnecting from pieces of who you are can make it difficult to foster self-love. Sometimes it could even cause you harm. You may brush a few things under the rug with no apparent consequence, but if that becomes habitual, a heaping mound may develop over time and you may trip on your own creation.

The willingness to understand and embrace your genuine self is essential in self-love. Without self-exploration crucial components of who you are, such as your identity, values, and purpose, may not be known. On top of this, as a teen you can reflect on and understand yourself in a way you could not have done when you were younger.

Self-exploration is an important skill to develop that will help you now and in the years to come. While some aspects of who we are remain constant for long periods of time, we do tend to change over the years. Without self-exploration, you may risk becoming stagnant in your self-love journey.

What do you anticipate you will encounter in your self-exploration?

GETTING TO KNOW YOU

Take some time to get to know you. Ask yourself the following questions in order to delve a bit deeper into your self-knowledge.

1. What is my favorite color?

2. What is my favorite band?

3. Who is my favorite artist?

4. What is my favorite book?

5. What is my favorite movie?

6. What is my favorite food?

7. What is my favorite animal?

8. What do I like to do for fun?

9. If I had only one wish, what would it be?

10. What is my proudest accomplishment?

11. Who do I love?

12. What do I want to try?

13. What am I ashamed of?

14. What am I worried about?

15. Where do I feel safest?

16. If I wasn't afraid I would...

17. When I'm feeling down I like to...

18. I know I'm stressed when...

19. My favorite thing about the world is...

20. What do I do to practice self-love?

21. What is my happiest memory?

22. What am I passionate about?

THE INDEPENDENT INTERVIEW

In the Getting to Know You activity on page 34, you may have noticed that some questions were easier to complete than others. Some questions may have even caused other questions to pop up in your mind. Here is your chance to continue that exploration. You can delve a bit deeper by asking yourself questions and allowing yourself time to reflect and answer them. The inspiration for the questions you select may have been sparked by the questions starting on page 34, or by something else altogether. Choose whatever topic comes to mind. Allow new questions to come up without judgment. Allow yourself to be curious and open to learning more about who you are. If you open your mind and heart, you will be able to improve your self-knowledge.

QUESTIONS	ANSWERS

MY STORY

A method of exploration is sharing your story. Exploring your personal narrative allows you to highlight and understand your history and how it influences who you are today. Key moments, such as milestones and lessons learned, are important to note as they have shaped who you are today and may continue to impact you for the rest of your life.

Use the prompts below to detail your narrative.

When I was born...

When I was younger I enjoyed...

Some of my challenges included...

My favorite memory is...

Some hard times included...

I was able to grow by...

I've learned...

Use this space to share important parts of your story that you did not get to share above.

Since self-exploration is an ongoing process, your narrative will continue. Use the prompts below to explore your future story.

In the future, I hope to learn...

____

____

____

____

I hope to have the opportunity to...

____

____

____

____

I wish that...

____

____

____

____

MY MISSION STATEMENT

"Those who have a 'why' to live can bear with almost any 'how.'"

—Nietzsche

Reflecting on your narrative helps you to connect to who you are and who you wish to be. A mission statement allows you to thread together the past and future. You are at a key time in your life in which your aspirations for the future can help you to recognize your personal mission. In doing so, you will better understand your identity, begin to develop a sense of purpose, and improve your overall happiness.

Here are prompts to assist you in exploring your personal purpose. Use the space to brainstorm and create your mission statement.

- What makes you happiest?
- When was a time that you felt purposeful?
- When do you feel most fulfilled?
- What do you want to accomplish?
- What type of life would you like to live?
- How do you want people to describe you?

CULTURAL EXPLORATION

"Our diversity is our strength. What a dull and pointless life it would be if everyone was the same."

—Angelina Jolie

One way to strengthen your self-knowledge is to learn about your culture. We tend to limit our view of culture. Many times we define ourselves by a sole category such as race or gender. But in reality, the concept of culture is much broader. Although you may have similarities to those in your family, community, or country, your cultural composition is unique to you.

Below are some common cultural domains. Take a moment to reflect on your identity for each segment. How does each part affect you?

- Age/Generation
- Ability/Disability Status
- Religious or Spiritual Beliefs
- Socioeconomic Status
- Sexual Orientation
- Nationality
- Gender
- Languages
- Teams/Clubs
- Interests

Key aspects of your culture may be encapsulated in the model above. However, your culture may include additional categories. This may include the town you are from, the groups you belong you, and the social roles that you fulfill.

What are some of the additional domains of your culture?

INNER CONFLICT

*"Happiness is when what you think, what you say,
and what you do are in harmony."*

—Mahatma Gandhi

By this point you may have learned a bit more about who you are. Though you are still the same person, the way you are reflecting may be changing. You may have shed light on pieces of yourself that are consistent with one another, but it is also possible that your exploration highlighted ways in which you may have dissonance, or a mismatch of thoughts, feelings, beliefs, values, experiences, or behaviors causing inner conflict.

In order to give yourself the love you deserve, you must first recognize when this inner conflict occurs. As like poles of two magnets, these forces may repel and cause you unhappiness.

One of the benefits of self-exploration is it allows you to bring these concerns to the surface. Then, you must work toward reducing the tension. You have the power to transform areas of dissonance into congruence, areas that match. When your thoughts, feelings, beliefs, values, experiences, and behaviors align, it is easier to provide yourself with self-love.

Here are some examples of how some other teens are experiencing dissonance. For each example, share your suggestion of how the inner conflict could be resolved.

Selena values honesty and trust but cheated on the last history test.

___

___

Jean is hurt to learn that her friends have been talking about her behind her back, but she also tends to gossip with others.

___

___

Raphael is very religious, but he has not prayed in months.

___

___

Alex is very dedicated to soccer but has missed multiple practices.

EXPLORING INNER CONFLICT

Take a moment to consider an inner conflict you may have. Place the opposing factors in the boxes below.

When you address an inner conflict, there are three points to consider. To practice, use the inner conflict you noted above to explore the following prompts:

1. Where does this conflict arise from?

2. How does this conflict affect me?

3. How can I take charge to achieve congruence?

CREATIVE EXPLORATION

In this chapter you have done a bit of deep thinking. Now it's time to unleash your creative side. Without any words, use the space below to illustrate who you are. This may include metaphors, symbols, or details you learned about yourself through self-exploration.

SELF-EXPLORATION CHAPTER REFLECTION

CHAPTER 4

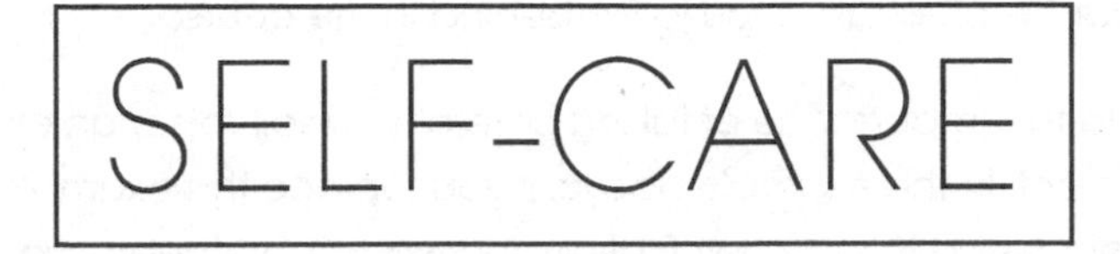

SELF-CARE

"There is only one corner of the universe you can be certain of improving, and that's your own self."

—Aldous Huxley

Self-care is a continuous process of considering and tending to your needs. It is a holistic process that we all need. When you practice self-care you can improve your presence, engagement, wellness, and self-love. On the other hand, when you neglect your needs, these areas may suffer over time. For example, you may notice increases in anxiety, distractibility, anger, and fatigue. You may also experience reductions in sleep quality, relationship satisfaction, self-esteem, empathy, and compassion. Ongoing exposure to stress without proper self-care can put you at risk for serious consequences such as depression and heart disease. Therefore, self-care is an essential self-loving practice.

Sometimes people mistake self-care as a singular skill, or a small set of habits. Instead, self-care includes a wide variety of tasks tailored to meet your diverse needs. Common dimensions of self-care include physical, creative, spiritual, natural, social, and personal. Examples of self-care activities include getting adequate sleep, practicing mindfulness, taking part in hobbies, and meditation.

As a preventative measure, self-care helps you to implement strategies prior to being faced with challenges. As a coping skill, self-care helps you to recognize when a new need calls for your attention. As an ongoing process, self-care helps you to develop resilience and compassion for yourself in your overall journey of self-love.

Oftentimes, self-care can be easier said than done. The intention to take care of your needs can sometimes be difficult to put into action. You might try to use similar self-care strategies that work for others, but self-care tends to vary from person to person. Just because a method works for someone else does not necessarily mean that it will work for you.

Self-care can be tricky. It is easy to forget to take care of yourself, particularly before taking care of your loved ones. When you are low on energy and short on time, you may be likely to give up your own needs for the sake of someone else. Over time this can be dangerous as it can create a habit of neglecting your wellness. Let's say that you love history, typically these classes tend to be your strong suit. Your fascination with the topic usually results in an easy A term after term. However, for the first time, you are struggling in your history course. You think about mentioning it to your parents, who are very supportive of you, but when you sit for dinner each night you hear your parents discuss how stressful their days were. You think to yourself, "It's not that important," and brush it off. While this may have been a seemingly considerate gesture, over time your confusion causes you to fall behind in the course.

It is helpful to demonstrate the importance of taking care of yourself to set an example and deter others you care for from self-neglect. In the example above, if you replace this example with a friend, over time would you encourage your friend to seek help? Likely you would. If someone you know was stranded on the side of the road because their car ran out of gas, would you empty your gas tank for them? Seems a little odd, right? You would likely use what you have to help that person get gas for their tank. Although kind, giving up all of your gas to help someone else creates a new problem altogether. Instead, the more effective way would be to fill your tank so you can better help someone fill theirs.

FILL YOUR CUP

How do you fill your self-care cup? Provide three examples below.

Example: *I go for walks.*

1. ______________________ 2. ______________________ 3. ______________________

Let's take this a little deeper. Why do you turn to these methods?

Example: *I go for walks to clear my mind, to take a break, to listen to music, to breathe the fresh air outdoors, and to stay active.*

1. ______________________ 2. ______________________ 3. ______________________

When you follow through with these examples, how do you feel?

Example: *After a walk I feel refreshed and I can focus better.*

1. ______________ 2. ______________ 3. ______________

When you lack the time or energy to follow through with these examples, do you notice a difference?

Example: *When I don't get to walk often I start to lose focus on things because walking is my favorite way to take a break.*

1. ______________ 2. ______________ 3. ______________

YOUR WELLNESS

When you hear the term "wellness," what comes to mind?

Did your definition include physical well-being? If it did, that is a common response. But it is important to realize that wellness is not one-dimensional. Consider these questions about wellness:

Do you feel your best when you set aside time for your friends and family?

____

Do you feel healthy when you are eating nutritious meals?

____

Do you feel happy when you pray to a higher power?

____

Do you feel balanced when you spend time in nature?

____

Do you feel healthy when you are at peace with the people around you?

____

If you answered yes to any of these questions, you might realize that your health is more than just physical wellness. Knowing the multifaceted aspects of wellness helps you to recognize the various ways you can foster your well-being and improve your self-love.

YOUR WELLNESS DOMAINS

Wellness domains are not the same for everyone. Let's take a moment to try to find the key areas of wellness that are important for your well-being. Circle the ones that resonate with you. You may add domains that are unique to your wellness that are not listed.

Community	Hobbies	Fitness and Exercise
Creative	Intellectual	Spiritual
Cultural	Personal Relationships	Work
Educational	Future Planning	________
Emotional	Love	________
Family	Mental	________
Financial	Nature	________
Friendship	Nutrition	________

Having a clear understanding of your wellness domains will help you to foster your well-being. Using the words you brainstormed on the previous page, try to lump like items to help you highlight a specific wellness domain.

For example, if you listed nutrition, exercise, and stretching you might want to categorize those into "physical." If you listed walks, hiking, and swimming, you might want to categorize those into "nature."

Try to form somewhere between four to eight categories.

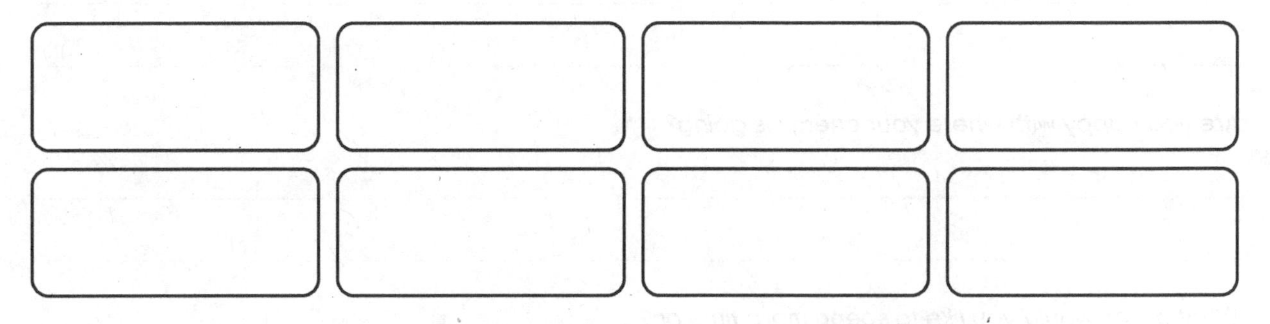

MY CURRENT WELLNESS

Our wellness is often limited by time. Now that you highlight that the domains above are important, you may aspire to practice all each week, but the reality is that there only 7 days in each week. Instead, it can be helpful to prioritize which aspects of your wellness are crucial to build often, how to balance the different aspects of your wellness, and how to align your wellness activities with the ratio of your needs.

Create a snapshot of your current wellness. Using the wellness categories that you clarified above, divide the categories into the pie chart below. Once you are finished, use the snapshot to answer the questions that follow.

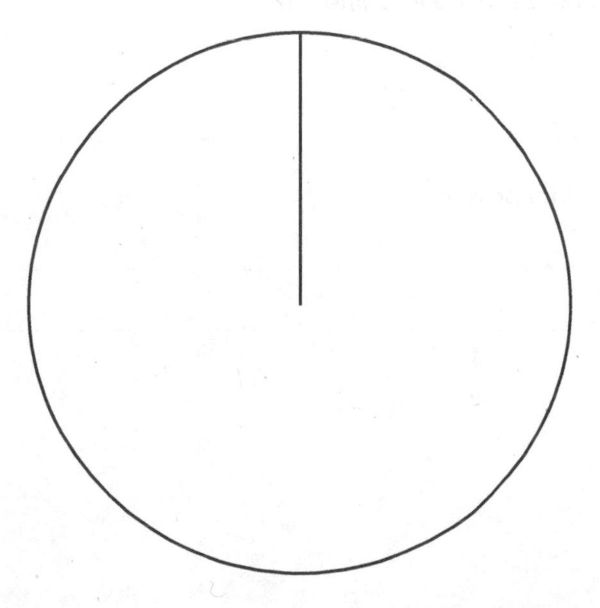

Are some parts of your time going to something beyond your wellness?

If so, is that acceptable for you?

Are you happy with where your energy is going?

What areas would you like to spend more time on?

How can you do that?

Are there areas you would like to spend less time on?

What do you need to make that possible?

CURRENT AND GOAL

"You can't cross the sea merely by standing and staring at the water."
—Rabindranath Tagore

Considering your reflection from My Current Wellness (page 51), what would you want your wellness to look like? Use your wellness categories and illustrate what you would like your division to look like in the chart below. Once you are finished, use the snapshot to answer the questions that follow.

What are your thoughts about your future wellness?

Did your categories remain the same as what was in your current wellness or did you notice a change?

What can help you to take steps toward making your ideal wellness realistic in the future?

Are there some challenges to achieving this?

STRIVING FOR BALANCE

In order to shift from your current snapshot to your ideal wellness, changes are necessary. Since time is a limited resource, when one domain changes it may cause a shift in at least one other domain. For example, you may notice that in order to acquire your ideal wellness you need to make more time for yourself. Related, you may observe that the social piece of your wellness is bigger in your current wellness than is needed in your ideal wellness. Hence, you may try to adjust by taking time from your social domain to fuel your personal wellness.

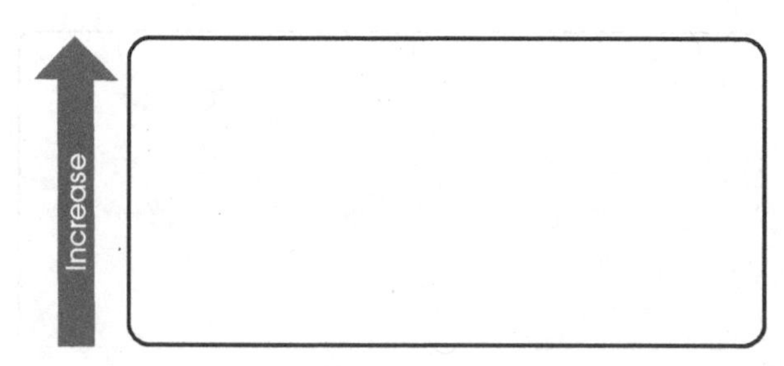

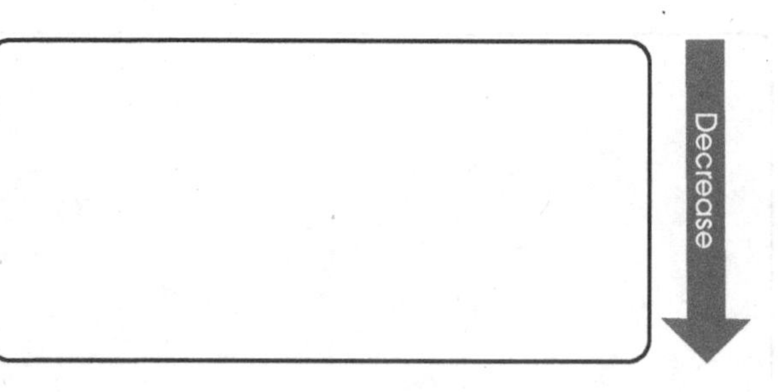

100 SELF-CARE STRATEGIES

Self-care strategies are the various skills that you use to tend to your needs. While we all need self-care, since our definitions of wellness differ, the methods that work for you may differ from others. It is helpful to attune the variety of needs you may have to select skills that work specifically for each. Having a variety of strategies helps you to diversify your self-care, and helps you to avoid becoming dependent on one method.

Example: Zara has been trying to better manage her anxiety. As a part of her efforts, she has been working on building her self-care toolkit. She has found that mindful coloring, crafting, and writing are her favorite skills. These help her to calm down and unwind after a hectic day. She has even created an actual box in her room where she keeps these items. One day at school she overhears a few classmates snickering about her. She tries to ignore it but becomes anxious and concerned. Without her box in that moment, she cannot practice some much-needed self-care. Although Zara has done an excellent job building her self-care, she would benefit from continuing to diversify her skills for different contexts.

Here is a list of 100 self-care strategies to help you get started.

- Circle all of the examples that have helped you in the past.
- Place a star next to all of the examples that you have not yet tried, but would like to try to help improve your wellness.
- Draw a line through the strategies that you know are not for you.

Affirmations
Attend a concert
Attend a sporting event
Bake
Breathe deeply
Call a helpline
Call an old friend
Clean
Color
Cook
Craft
Create an affirmation
Create boundaries
Dance
De-clutter
Donate
Do something nice for someone else
Do yoga
Draw
Eat a healthy meal
Exercise
Embrace silence
Forgive someone
Get a massage
Get a manicure
Get a pedicure
Give a compliment
Give a hug
Go outside
Go to the beach
Go to therapy
Groom yourself
Hydrate
Journal
Knit
Light a candle
Light incense
Listen to music
Listen to a podcast
Listen to your favorite song
Look at old photos
Look at the sky
Make a gratitude list
Make a positivity playlist
Make a mandala
Make travel plans
Meditate
Meet a friend
Nap
Organize
Paint
Plan a trip
Plant
Play a game
Play a sport
Play an instrument
Play video games
Play with a pet
Practice assertiveness
Practice mindfulness
Pray
Read
Rearrange furniture
Rest
Run
Say no to negativity
Set a goal
Sew
Sing
Smile
Solve a puzzle
Spend time in nature
Spend time with positive people
Stretch
Study
Take a bath
Take a break
Take a mental health day
Take pictures
Take a shower
Take your vitamins
Think positively
Try a DIY project
Try a new recipe
Unplug from social media
Use a fidget toy
Use essential oils
Hold an ice cube to manage anger
Use visualization
Volunteer
Walk
Watch funny videos
Watch the sunset
Watch your favorite movie
Watch your favorite show
Work
Write a letter
Write a poem
Write a song
Write a story

CREATIVE SELF-CARE

"Creativity is intelligence having fun."

—Albert Einstein

Although everyone can benefit from self-care, not everyone benefits from the same self-care strategies. The 100 Self-Care Strategies you explored on page 54 are common ways that people tend to their needs; however, it can be helpful to get creative with your self-care. Honor your uniqueness and allow yourself to be creative. This can help you find ways that work for you beyond the common self-care strategies. In addition, making an active effort to infuse your creativity into regular self-care practice can help you to foster your well-being.

- Someone who loves understanding how things work could find tinkering with a gadget peaceful and enjoyable.
- Someone who enjoys making pottery may find holding clay to be more calming than someone who does not.
- Someone who loves seeking adventure could find it fulfilling to check off ziplining from their bucket list.

These examples are personalized. Although others could enjoy them too, they're not necessarily common coping mechanisms but still just as helpful.

Reflect on who you are. See page 40, My Mission Statement, for some perspective.

What are the creative ways that you may cope?

SELF-CARE DONE RIGHT

Let's take a moment to zoom into your self-care strategies. It's important to self-reflect and assure that you are using quality skills to help you cope.

- There's such a thing as too much self-care. For example, a massage can be a helpful way to relax and soothe your body; however, multiple massages in a short time can be expensive and counterproductive.
- Some self-care strategies may be healthy for someone else, but may be unhealthy for you. For example, if you have been diagnosed with diabetes, you might need to be more careful than others when it comes to consuming sweets.
- Some strategies differ in quality depending on how someone uses them. For example, video games can be a positive strategy to feel a sense of critical thinking, teamwork, and accomplishment; however, playing video games alone for hours may not be as productive.
- Using the 100 Self-Care Strategies on page 54, place the skills in the corresponding column below. You may also add additional skills beyond the list. Some methods may be clearly positive, others may be obviously negative, and some may have the potential to be both. If you can explain why the skill goes into that category, this will help you be more mindful of your self-care selection in times of need.

POSITIVE	CONDITIONAL	NEGATIVE
Example: *Meditating always helps me to center myself. Even if I am short on time, a simple breathing meditation helps.*	Example: *Video games help me spend time with my friends but when I spend too much time it can be unhelpful.*	Example: *Sometimes when I'm angry I want to scream at the person who bothered me, but even though this releases my anger in the moment I feel even worse after.*

MY WELLNESS PLAN

Now, create a plan to help you balance your wellness. Use the examples on the previous page or think about all of the possible things you can do to fill each wellness slice. You don't need to master meditation hour or escape to an island paradise to achieve balance. Of course, those can be considered; however, brainstorm tangible tasks that you can easily do in your everyday life to boost your wellness domains. Bigger items are encouraged, but remember that small efforts can add up as well.

Divide the space for each wellness domain. List all of the strategies you could use to fuel that dimension of wellness. You may use the strategies noted on page 54, but I also encourage you to self-reflect and consider strategies that are specific to you as well.

Now that you have a variety of ways to fuel your wellness, think about how to incorporate these aspects of wellness into your everyday life. Try to place the strategies from above in their corresponding section.

These are the things I would like to do for my wellness...

Daily:

____

____

Twice a week:

____

____

Weekly:

____

____

Every other week:

____

____

Monthly:

____

____

At least once per season:

____

____

At least once a year:

____

____

LISTENING TO YOUR EMOTIONS

It is important to have a healthy connection to your emotions. However, we often minimize the power of our emotions. Many times we view them as distracting, ignore them, and believe that they are unhelpful. In reality, feelings can serve as practical, powerful signals to help you foster your self-love (See page 20, Emotional Awareness.)

Like waves in an ocean, emotions come and go. If you pay attention to them, you can adjust accordingly and take better care of yourself. When you are at the beach, if you don't pay attention when you are in the water, a wave may rush over you. Even if you do see that a wave is coming your way, it makes no sense to dig your feet into the sand and try to stand your ground. Instead, you ride the wave. Before long, it will be gone.

Instead of ignoring or fighting against your feelings, you need to learn to work with them. All feelings, positive or negative, have a purpose. For example, when you are joyful, your feeling tells you that things are going well in that moment. On the other hand, when you are anxious, that may be a sign that something is wrong and you may need to adjust. Learning the reasons emotions arise can help us to better care for ourselves.

When it comes to self-care, you may find that certain skills work better for some emotions over others. Listening to your emotions may help you to choose the appropriate coping skill in that moment. You wouldn't use a hammer when you need a screwdriver, and coping skills may also have specific purposes. Take the time to equip yourself with effective coping skills to be well aware, prepared, and more likely to cope effectively.

Find a self-care strategy that would be particularly helpful for each emotion below.

Example: *If you know that texting your BFF helps to lift your spirits, then you may wish to put "text BFF" in the "Sad" section.*

Sad	Stupid	Jealous	Ashamed

Inferior	Sleepy	Annoyed	Anxious
Bored	Hurt	Discouraged	Disgusted

When you're not sure how you feel, thinking about how you want to feel can help you select the appropriate coping skill.

Place a corresponding coping skill in each box below.

Example: *If you know that taking a warm water bath helps to calm you, then you may wish to put "take a bath" in the "Relaxed" section.*

Relaxed	Thankful	Confident	Valuable

Satisfied	Creative	Playful	Daring
Aware	Respected	Amused	Proud

Did you have a hard time filling in all of the spaces? If you found yourself stuck, allow the blank space to motivate you. Keep your mind and heart open to coping skills that may fit the blank domains and fill them in when you become familiar with them.

COPING TOOLKIT

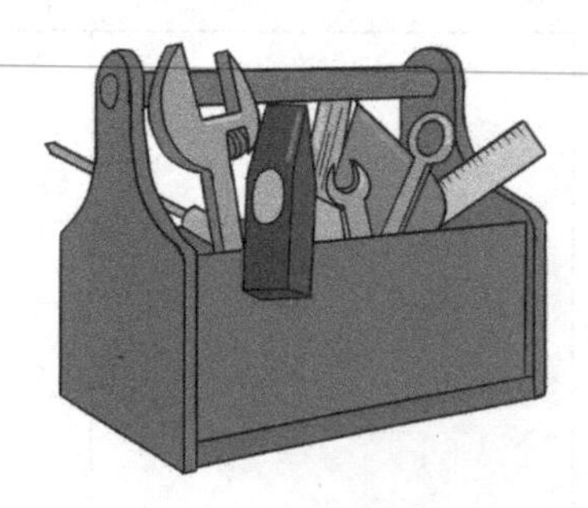

Challenges are a normal part of life. While you can't avoid challenges, you're not helpless to them either. If you proactively work on your coping, you can be better prepared to handle those difficulties. One way you can do this is by building a coping kit with go-to coping skills that are effective for you.

By now, you have explored general self-care strategies and specific coping skills, and you may have even included some unique methods of your own. Use the space on the next page to remind yourself of all of the coping strategies that you've learned work for you over time.

Share any important details to help you use these skills when the time is needed.

Make a note of their purpose(s). As you journey through this workbook, you may learn more about your self-care over time. As you gain more tools, be sure to come back and add them here.

Example: *Deep breathing. This helps me when I am anxious, overhwhelmed, confused, and sad. This skill works best when I'm in a dark and comfortable space, but I can practice it anywhere.*

What types of tools would you like to add to your kit?

What are your favorite coping skills?

What coping skills can you use when you are short on time?

What coping skills can you use by yourself?

What coping skills can you use without spending any money?

MANDALA

You might associate coloring with your childhood years; however, the calming power of this art can benefit any age. Doodling and coloring are common forms of self-care. Mandalas, such as the one below, are intricate geometric figures that are seen in various cultures across the globe. The mindful practice of filling in these dynamic designs can be particularly helpful to return to equilibrium.

Grab ahold of three or more of your favorite coloring utensils and set aside a few minutes to immerse in the mandala below. Focus solely on the figure. It is normal for outside thoughts to pop up. Notice them as they arise and set them aside for a moment so you can continue with your task.

JOURNALING

Journaling is a form of reflective writing. There are different types of journaling strategies that allow you to explore your thoughts, feelings, and behaviors without judgment. Some methods can help you to experience a brief escape from reality while others engage you to resolve deep conflicts.

You can take each activity in this book a step further by choosing to journal afterword. You have already had a few chances to try journaling in this workbook. In Chapter 2, Self-Awareness (page 18), you had the opportunity to utilize an open-ended journal prompt. Also, at the end of each chapter you have had the opportunity to use journaling to review and reflect on the topics in each section. Many of the activities call for a small, succinct reflection. Opportunities to deepen your reflection through journaling are provided in the margins throughout the workbook.

As you can see, journaling methods can range from general to specific. Here are a few examples:

Open-ended: This type of journaling is intentionally broad to allow for enhanced exploration. For example, you may choose to reflect on self-love without constraining your exploration to a specific prompt. This approach allows your mind to freely wander. Without limitations, you may encounter thoughts and feelings that you may not have recognized otherwise.

Release: Also known as a stream-of-consciousness prompt, this is a partially open-ended journal in which you intentionally purge any and every thought that comes to mind in that given moment. Yes, even the thought "I don't have any more thoughts" gets released in the writing if it comes to mind. This style is often effective with a timer set for a short amount of time. If you've had a heated argument with someone but need to go back to class, you may use this method to release and help you to reset in time for class.

Review: Similar to the prompts at the end of each chapter in this book, a review prompt can help you assess a particular event, theme, or topic. While doing so, you are able to revisit the topic and take your reflection deeper. This type of journal is commonly used at the end of the day. For example, you may wish to reflect daily on your self-care practices.

Plan: A planning journal allows you to brainstorm your hopes and dreams. In addition, you can explore possible methods to help you tangibly achieve them. This method works well in conjunction with the review style of journaling, as you can reflect on what has occurred and how to continue to improve over time.

Emotion: It's important to be in tune with your emotions, but they can be difficult to pinpoint in the moment. Reflecting can help you to understand them better. An emotion journal allows you to explore your feelings by recognizing emotions that have come to the surface, what has triggered them, and how you can manage them. This is also helpful in situations in which multiple complicated emotions arise, or when you are trying to empathize with and understand someone else's emotional experience in order to better communicate.

Gratitude: A gratitude journal allows you to explore reasons you are thankful. This type of writing generally consists of open-ended prompts that are broadly focused on what you are thankful for. However, you may choose to explore specific realms of gratitude. For example, for one entry you could reflect on things you are grateful to have achieved and in another you could focus on the people you are grateful to have in your life.

What type of journaling do you enjoy?

____

____

____

____

____

MY COMFORT ZONE

Your environment can play an important role in your self-care. It is helpful to consider what type of setting works well for your wellness. In your safe space you feel comfortable and relaxed. In your comfort zone you are able to let your guard down and be vulnerable. In this environment you are likely to think more clearly and feel more attuned to who you are. You may already have a place in mind, or you may have to create a comfort zone. In the space below, sketch your safe space.

Some common characteristics of a comfort zone:

- Fresh air
- Music
- Cozy blanket
- Candle
- Plush pillow

SELF-LOVE DATE

"To love oneself is the beginning of a lifelong romance."
—Oscar Wilde

In order to love others, we must first learn to love ourselves. When we think of dating, an image of two people spending quality time to show their shared appreciation may come to mind. But could you do this for yourself?

Taking the time to plan a date for yourself shows that you recognize and respect your self-worth. While it is important to be kind and caring to others, it is especially helpful to begin that practice with yourself. To foster your self-love, treat yourself the way you treat the special people in your life. Just as you wouldn't think twice about spending the time, energy, and effort to show appreciation for a loved one, you can do the same for yourself. When you treat yourself with love, you help others learn how to love you as well.

Consider your wellness and how you receive love. Take a moment to plan a date just for you.

Where would you go?

____

____

What would you like to do?

____

____

____

How much time would you need?

____

____

How do you need to prepare?

____

____

____

When would you go?

Share other important details about your Self-Love Date:

EXPLORING MY SUPPORT SYSTEM

Your social support system is made up of the people you can turn to for help, who care for you, and who may signal your self-care necessities when they see something in your blind spot. These are the people who encourage, assist, guide, and motivate you along your self-love journey. Positive people provide for a wealth of support for self-care. While they are generally a positive influence on your wellness, they become a priceless resource when you are in a time of need.

Begin to explore your support system in the space below. List all of the people that have or can help to support your self-love.

BORING SELF-CARE

A common misconception is that all self-care is fun. There are many enjoyable, and sometimes even exciting, elements in self-care. Self-care is the self-loving action of tending to your needs, and not all needs are thrilling. However, recognizing these responsibilities as acts of self-love can help you expand the scope of your self-care practice. While these strategies may be boring, they are essential and should not be overlooked.

List the self-care strategies that may bore you, but are essential.

SELF-CARE STRATEGY	THIS IS IMPORTANT BECAUSE...
Example: Doing my laundry	Doing laundry is annoying. But I know that when it's done I feel a sense of accomplishment. I get to wear my favorite clothes, and this boosts my mood too. It's also nice when my room isn't cluttered and gross.

CHALLENGING SELF-CARE

"Do the difficult things while they are easy and do the great things while they are small. A journey of a thousand miles must begin with a single step."

—Lao Tzu

Not all parts of self-care are pleasant, but at the end of the day, they are all positive.

Some aspects of self-care are downright difficult. However, the following difficult pieces of self-care have a substantial positive impact on your wellness.

It is important to shed light on these difficult aspects of self-care in order to hold ourselves accountable to pursue them.

Examples of challenging self-care:

- Creating limits for yourself
- Confronting someone who consistently hurts you
- Cutting ties with a toxic friend

What are the challenging tasks in your self-care?

____

____

____

____

What do you need to empower you to tackle these difficult duties?

____

____

____

____

SELF-CARE CHAPTER REFLECTION

CHAPTER 5

SELF-ESTEEM

How would you define self-esteem? We all know that having healthy self-esteem is essential, but it's often confused with similar terms such as confidence, efficacy, and worth. Although these terms are related, it is important to recognize what self-esteem is by itself.

Your self-esteem is how you view your worth, and how you think, feel, and act because of your assessment. It consists of beliefs you hold about yourself. In essence, it is a judgment that you derive in reference to your personal value. When you have low self-esteem you tend to maintain a poor view of yourself. On the other hand, a high self-esteem demonstrates a strong sense of worthiness. Low self-esteem is associated with stress, depression, prejudice, materialism, relationship insecurity, and poor coping. Low self-esteem is a known risk factor in the development of mental health problems such as eating disorders, anxiety, and depression.

Another misunderstanding is that high self-esteem is often seen to be the gold standard. In reality, a healthy sense of esteem may fluctuate. While individuals with low self-esteem are often more vulnerable, on the opposite end of the spectrum, an individual with extraordinarily high self-esteem could be defensive and irrational.

Knowing this detail is important when trying to build and monitor a healthy sense of self-esteem.

The teenage years are a pivotal time for fostering self-esteem. As noted on page 38, key milestones in this time make a healthy self-esteem important. Also, self-esteem now helps to set the foundation for your adult years ahead. However, self-esteem is not only important during adolescence. Self-esteem is important to build as you are growing up, and it will continue to influence you throughout your life.

Since self-esteem is essential in self-love, it is important to be clear on what it actually entails, to distinguish it from similar concepts and to dispel false associations. Fostering your self-esteem helps you to better understand yourself, develop a healthier sense of identity, and foster healthier relationships with others. Furthermore, in honoring your worth in your purest form, you respect the value of others as well. Hence, self-esteem can be a helpful factor in your personal journey of self-love, yet the benefits can have a broader impact on the world around you.

Now that we have clarified what self-esteem is, how would you assess your self-esteem at this current time?

Has your self-esteem differed in the past?

What is a positive part of your self-esteem?

How could you improve your self-esteem?

ACKNOWLEDGING MY WORTH

"The world needs a sense of worth, and it will achieve it only by its people feeling that they are worthwhile."

—Fred Rogers

Take a moment and consider your worth. As discussed in What Self-Love Isn't (page 10), acknowledging your self-worth does not make you prideful, selfish, or entitled. Strip away your titles, achievements, and experiences. You, as a human being, are worthy. Just as you are, you are valid, important, and enough.

I am worthy of...

1. ______________________
2. ______________________
3. ______________________
4. ______________________
5. ______________________
6. ______________________
7. ______________________
8. ______________________
9. ______________________
10. ______________________
11. ______________________
12. ______________________
13. ______________________
14. ______________________
15. ______________________
16. ______________________
17. ______________________
18. ______________________
19. ______________________
20. ______________________

What was it like to explore your self-worth?

What was easy about writing the list above?

What did you find challenging?

MY PERSONAL QUALITIES

We typically think about ourselves in three ways: positive, negative, or neutral. You may not realize when your mental tone shifts from one the other. Since this is difficult to recognize, your thoughts may shift to the negative without you even realizing. On top of this, thinking negatively can become a habit.

Think about your self-evaluations like a self-love bank account. When you think negatively about yourself you withdraw from your account; on the other hand, positive thoughts can enhance your balance. Recognizing these internal transactions is helpful to heighten your awareness and empower you to monitor your self-love.

POSITIVE, NEGATIVE, OR NEUTRAL

Take a moment to list your personal attributes. This can include adjectives that describe personality, appearance, habits, interests, roles, and experiences. Place the characteristic in the appropriate column. For example, you may place optimistic in positive, talkative in neutral, and bossy in negative. Keep in mind that your categories should be based on your own perspectives. For example, while others may see being talkative as a skill, others may see it as negative; what matters the most is that you may view it as both.

POSITIVE	NEUTRAL	NEGATIVE

CONFIDENT PEOPLE

Confidence can be defined as the trust you have in yourself. Can you think of three people that you believe have a large amount of self-trust?

On a scale of 1 to 10 with one being little to no confidence and 10 being as confident as possible, place a star to rate the confidence level of each person you select.

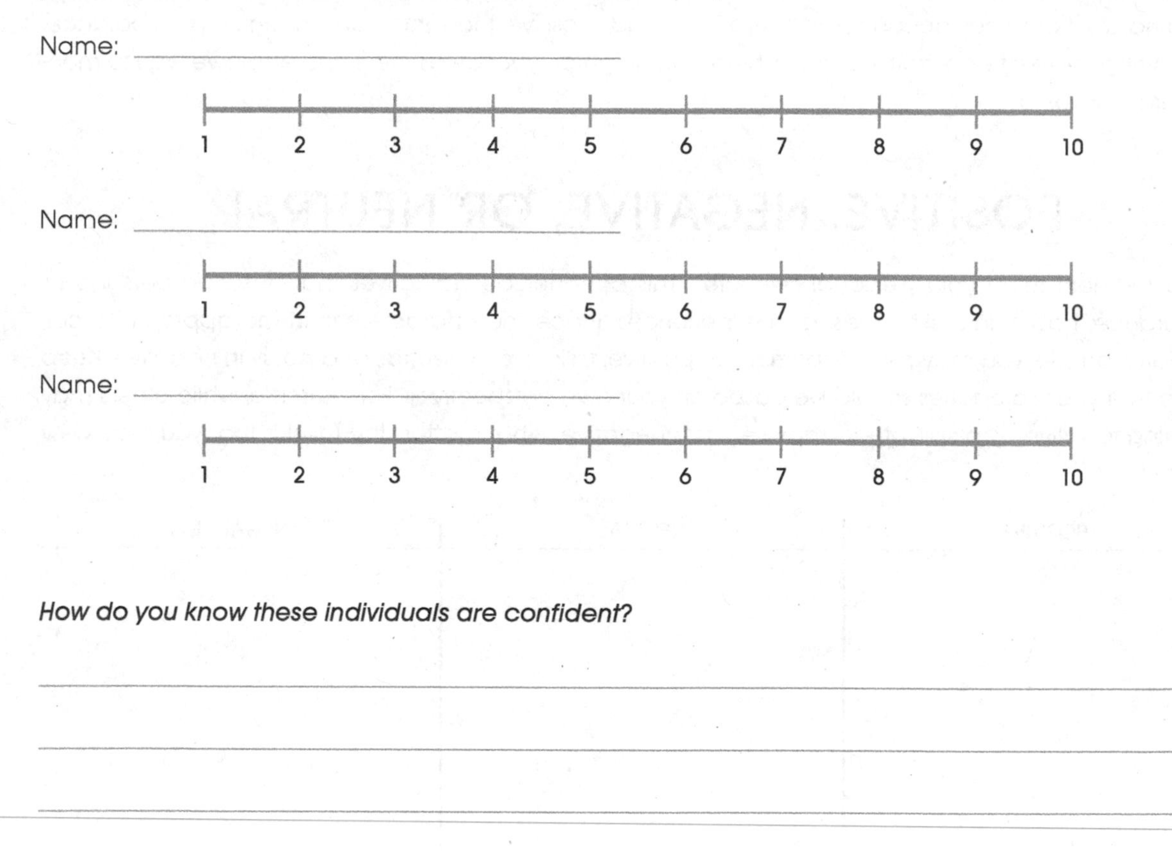

How do you know these individuals are confident?

What do you believe helps them to have high confidence?

What do you believe hinders their confidence?

Thinking about confident people that you admire can help you to view confidence in an inspirational and nonthreatening way. Observing confidence in people you know can help you to set examples for yourself. Also, examining what builds their confidence can allow you to consider methods to improve your own self-confidence.

EXPLORING MY CONFIDENCE

"Go confidently in the direction of your dreams. Live the life you have imagined."

—Henry David Thoreau

Think about a time in your past in which you did not trust yourself. Describe that event below.	Think about a time in your past in which you trusted yourself. Describe that event below.
Looking back, did you have any reasons to trust yourself?	Looking back, what reasons did you have to trust yourself?

Did anything stand in your way at the time?	Did anything cause your trust to waver?

If you compare and contrast these events, what do you notice?

HOW CONFIDENT AM I?

How confident are you in this present moment? Circle your selected number on the scale of 1 to 10 below, with 1 being little to no confidence and 10 being as confident as possible.

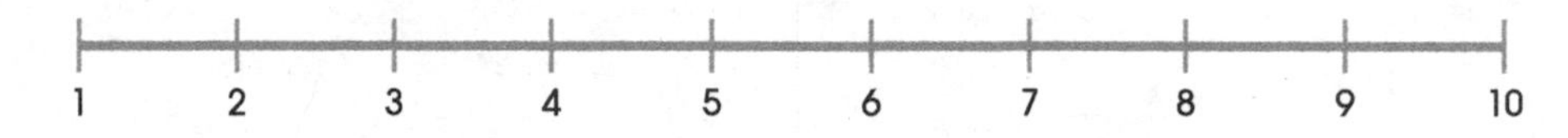

How did you decide on this number?

Are you happy with this number?

What could make this number decrease?

What could make this number increase?

UNDERSTANDING SELF-EFFICACY

"It always seems impossible until it's done."

—Nelson Mandela

When exploring your confidence you may have found it difficult to pick a number from 1 to 10. That's because this prompt may have expanded your self-awareness. Sometimes it can be hard to connect to your inner voice. Self-esteem is a personal assessment, but you may have struggled to separate yourself from outside influences. On top of this, you may have recognized how broad confidence can be. You might have thought, "Confident in what?" or found that your confidence varies by topic. For example, you might be confident in a sport you enjoy, but less confident in a sport that you have not yet tried.

Another way to assess at your confidence, or self-trust, is to consider your belief in your abilities, otherwise known as self-efficacy. No one is perfect, and regardless of your hard work, intentions, and effort, you can't do it all. We all have both strengths and weaknesses. Using the angle of self-efficacy allows you to better understand your skill sets, deficits, and all that lies in between.

Self-efficacy allows us to honor our talents. Acknowledging the areas in which you may be lacking through the lens of efficacy rather than confidence allows for a flexible way of seeing yourself. For example, you might have low self-efficacy about your ability to run a marathon tomorrow and to complete it within 4 hours and 20 minutes. This does not mean that running a marathon in 4 hours and 20 minutes is impossible, it just means that if you were not previously training for such an endeavor, it would be a bit absurd to set such a standard. Your confidence may be low, but recognizing it is understandable that you do not have certain abilities needed to take on this feat tomorrow is a healthier perspective. On the other hand, if you have coincidentally been training for a marathon for months, previously completed a marathon in a similar time frame, and just so happen to have a race tomorrow, perhaps you may have high self-efficacy and confidence in this area.

MY SELF-EFFICACY

For each prompt below, rate your current self-efficacy. For each task, place a star along the line to indicate your level. Then, explain how you arrived at that assessment.

Drive a car

LOW .... HIGH

___

___

Write in cursive

LOW .... HIGH

___

___

Create a budget

LOW .... HIGH

___

___

Change a diaper

LOW .... HIGH

___

___

ROLE MODELS

A role model is someone whom you admire. Aspects of who they are align with who you are or who you wish to be. Role models authentically represent our values, beliefs, and/or interests in ways that are inspiring. They may demonstrate a healthy sense of self-efficacy, confidence, and self-esteem.

People you know can be helpful role models as you may ask them about their own self-love journey. For example, a friend that you believe has high self-esteem may be willing to discuss their path toward healthy self-esteem. From that conversation, you may be able to find insightful points to consider for your own process. A role model does not need to be limited to someone you know personally. Historical figures, fictional characters, and influential celebrities could have the potential to inspire you and assist you in boosting your self-esteem as well.

Explore your role models. Try to find at least one per category. Explain what draws you to each role model. Include what you have in common and what inspires you about that individual.

ACQUAINTANCE	HISTORICAL FIGURE	FICTIONAL CHARACTER	CELEBRITY

What self-esteem lessons can you learn from the individuals above?

MY INNER DIALOGUE

"All our dreams can come true, if we have the courage to pursue them."

—Walt Disney

In order to truly consider your esteem, confidence, and efficacy, you must be able to tune into your inner dialogue, or self-talk. Self-talk consists of the things you say to yourself. Self-talk is normal, and we all do it, but it's so common that we don't tend to pay it any attention. However, our inner dialogue can be a powerful influence on our ability to love ourselves.

Listening to your internal chatter can help you to notice your personal assessments. The messages included in your internal script may range from positive to negative. Like heavy weights, your negative self-talk could be dragging down your assessment of yourself. On the other hand, positive, helpful thoughts can help you to feel empowered and unrestrained. If you are attentive to your self-talk, you may be able to connect how it could be affecting your esteem, confidence, and efficacy, and ultimately, your self-love.

Some examples of negative self-talk:

- I'll never be able to be confident.
- I can't do anything right.
- No one likes to be around me.

Considering the examples above, what are some negative statements you have said to yourself?

____

____

____

____

____

____

____

As mentioned, inner chatter can go unnoticed. However, paying attention to our thoughts can help us to recognize when unacceptable negative thoughts are creating barriers to self-love. It can also empower us to transform these patterns into positive thoughts and foster self-love in the process.

It may be difficult to recognize your self-talk in this moment, but now you know that it is important to be attentive to your self-talk. As you continue your journey, you might notice negative self-talk that you previously overlooked. When you do, add those statements here.

UNHELPFUL THINKING

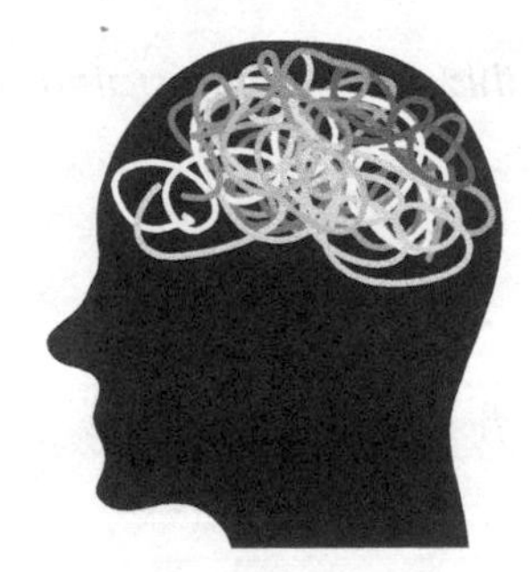

Sometimes negative self-talk doesn't make that much sense. It can be distorted or irrational. However, regardless of accuracy, negative self-talk can still influence your self-esteem. When you can recognize and challenge your negative self-talk, you may be able to avoid absorbing the negative consequences. If you focus on catching unhelpful statements, you have the opportunity to widen your perspective and alter your thinking.

Highlighting and transforming negative inner dialogue can be a self-loving practice.

The first step in addressing negative self-talk is to become aware that the given thought is indeed unhelpful.

CHALLENGING UNHELPFUL THINKING

"With the new day comes new strength and new thoughts."

—Eleanor Roosevelt

Self-awareness is key in recognizing when you may be experiencing distorted thoughts (see Self-Awareness on page 18). When you are unaware, you are unable to challenge your unhealthy thoughts. In the box below, provide an example of an unhealthy self-statement that has deeply affected you. If possible, try to choose a thought that you struggle to change that still affects you today.

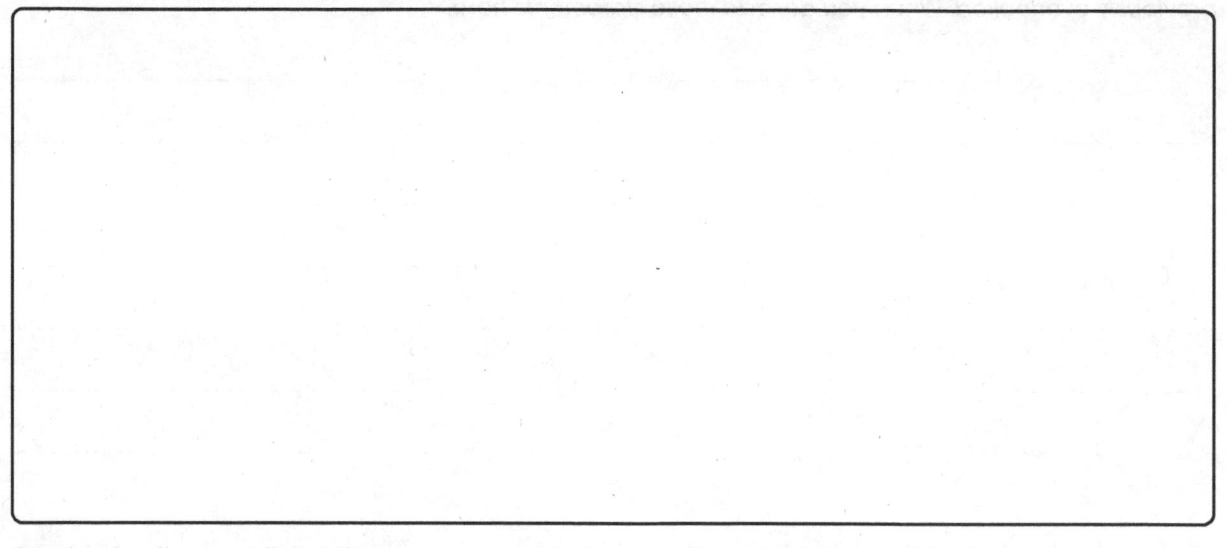

Considering the negative statement you provided, answer the following questions. They can help you to challenge your unhelpful thinking.

Is this a self-loving statement?

Is this thought helpful?

Is it in my control?

Am I blaming myself unnecessarily?

Am I holding myself to unrealistic standards?

Are there exceptions that I'm ignoring?

How likely is this?

Am I jumping to conclusions?

Am I taking this personally, when it may not be a personal matter?

Am I making assumptions?

How can I test my assumptions?

Could there be other perspectives?

How do I know that this thought is accurate?

What evidence do I have to support this thought?

What are other ways to think about it?

Is there someone I can seek feedback from to check the accuracy of this thought?

What would I say to a friend in this situation?

TRASH TOSS

Our internal messages may be influenced by messages from others. For example, if you are in a healthy friendship, your friend may share encouraging and supportive statements that you may absorb over time. On the other hand, if you are in an unhealthy friendship, their toxic and demeaning remarks may cause the quality of your self-talk to deteriorate.

You can't control others' statements, but you can consider when a message is helpful, consistent with who you are, and self-loving.

Take a moment to sort those statements. Think about statements you have been told from people around you. It can be particularly helpful to use statements that multiple people have shared. Consider if this statement is worthy of keeping since it helps to boost your self-esteem or if it needs to be tossed since it hinders your view of your worth.

When thinking about messages you have been told about yourself...

Which statements will you choose to keep?

____

____

How do these statements affect you?

____

____

What does this tell you about the relationship you have with the people who said these statements?

____

____

Which thoughts belong in the bin below?

____

____

How do these statements affect you?

____

____

What does this tell you about the relationship you have with the people who said these statements?

____

____

PETAL POWER: IMPROVING POSITIVE SELF-TALK

It's wonderful when you are able to counter your negative thinking with a positive thought, but it's even better when you can overpower the unhealthy statement with multiple healthy statements. The combination of healthier statements combine to create a powerful perspective.

Reflect on your inner dialogue and consider your commonly used negative statements. For each flower, place one example of negative self-talk in the center. Then, use the petals to brainstorm ways to counter that negative thought. You may find it helpful to consider the questions from Trash Toss/the previous activity.

Try your best to create positive and powerful perspectives that are infused with self-love!

BUILDING BLOCKS

You can increase your positive thoughts and improve your self-esteem by reflecting on your strengths, achievements, abilities, and successes.

Think of these thoughts as building blocks that help you to shape your self-esteem.

Use the prompts in the blocks below to help you construct a strong foundation for positive self-talk. Feel free to use the blank boxes to continue to create your own unique statements.

In the future I will...	People can count on me to...
I know I can trust myself to...	Even on my bad days I am still...
If I tried hard I could...	A pure strength of mine is...
Even though I didn't think I would succeed at the time, I am happy that I...	I know that I can...

I like that I...

I am good at...

I have been able to...

I am capable of...

I am proud that I...

After a lot of hard work I...

MOTIVATIONAL MESSAGES

We all experience hard days from time to time. On these days, our self-esteem could use a little extra boost. Motivational messages can help to fill this void by giving you inspiration when you need it most.

First, it can be helpful to reflect on what motivational messages resonate with you. Messages that you may find motivating can come from a variety of sources, such as words your loved ones have shared to encourage you, inspirational quotes, and affirmations.

You can use those words to spark your creativity. When it comes to self-love, it is particularly beneficial to craft motivational messages for you from you. Taking the time to proactively tailor a simple statement to help you step into your power on a difficult day is a practical and impactful act of self-love.

ENCOURAGERS

It's important to be kind to yourself when you need it the most. In times when you find yourself struggling, you have the ability help yourself through encouragement. Oftentimes these helpful statements come from other people who wish to encourage us in our journey, especially in the times that we become discouraged.

Think about the people in your life who have positively influenced you. These individuals may include your parents, family, friends, coaches, teachers, and so on.

What are some statements others have said to encourage you?

INSPIRATIONAL QUOTES

We do not need to know someone directly to be influenced by them. For example, consider the celebrities you may admire. When we relate to people such as leaders, scientists, authors, and musicians, we can be inspired by them without even ever meeting them. These influential individuals may have famous words that can help to motivate us during difficult days.

Here are a few examples of inspirational quotes:

"The future belongs to those who believe in the beauty of their dreams."

—Eleanor Roosevelt

"If I cannot do great things, I can do small things in a great way."

—Martin Luther King Jr.

"It always seems impossible until it's done."

—Nelson Mandela

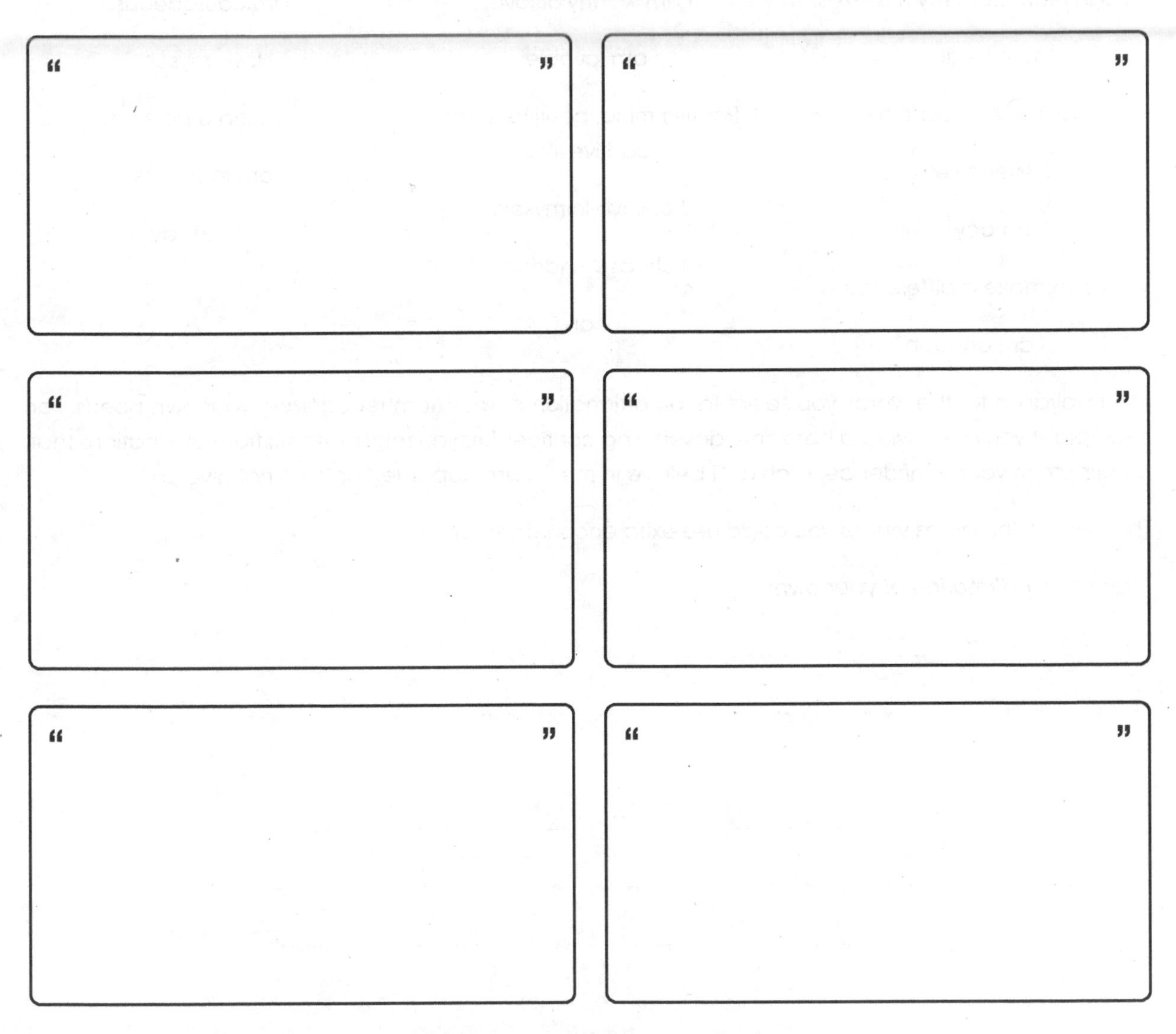

AFFIRMATIONS

Another specific type of motivational message is an affirmation.

Affirmations are practical, positive self-talk statements that can empower you and boost your self-esteem.

Affirmations are powerful because they are simple yet encouraging messages that resonate with you. These short sentences can serve as an encouraging nudge of self-love.

Here are some examples. Select the ones that resonate with you:

I can learn from my mistakes.

Life is beautiful.

Practice over perfection.

Never give up.

I am powerful.

I can make a difference.

I am enough.

I am worthy of love.

I am lovable.

Positive mind, positive heart, positive life.

I believe in myself.

I choose kindness.

I can.

I am courageous.

I love myself.

Anything is possible.

I am fortunate.

I am ready.

The inspiration for the words you select for an affirmation comes from recognizing your own needs. For example, if you are having a hard time developing confidence, you might benefit from affirmations that contribute to your confidence, such as "I believe in me," "I am capable," or "I will not give up."

Think about the areas where you could use extra encouragement.

Create an affirmation of your own:

Affirmations work best when you practice them. Each time you revisit your affirmation you reinforce its strength. Try to read your affirmation at least once a day. It can be helpful to come up with clever reminders. Maybe you would benefit from setting an alarm, changing your phone background, or placing sticky notes where you will see them. Use your creativity to come up with a fun way that works for you!

How you view yourself can greatly affect your self-love. Negative thoughts can taint your view of your worth and can serve as obstacles in promoting self-love. On the other hand, a positive mindset can help you to create a sturdy foundation to foster your self-loving practices.

SEND YOURSELF AN EMAIL

Now that you have had the opportunity to explore encouragers, inspirational quotes, and affirmations, take a moment and write yourself a short motivating email. Try to infuse the 3 types of messages to help boost your self-esteem.

SELF-ESTEEM CHAPTER REFLECTION

CHAPTER 6

SELF-KINDNESS

As children, we are taught the value of being kind. This worthwhile lesson helps us to learn how to be nice to others. The notion of being kind to yourself is often overlooked, and because of this, self-kindness is often overshadowed as a segment of self-love.

Self-kindness is the skill of being friendly to yourself, and it is equally important to being nice to others. You can learn and integrate self-kindness into your self-love practice as a teen and at any point in your life.

Self-kindness can include how you provide yourself with grace and comfort in times you need it most. It can also encompass your approach to a negative thought, feeling, prompt, or situation. For example, having the self-awareness to know you are exhausted at the end of the school week and making plans to rest and recuperate is a gesture of self-kindness.

You demonstrate self-kindness when you're faced with hurdles in your path and it's essential to be compassionate toward yourself rather than be judgmental or critical.

Self-kindness is the balance you strive for between being dedicated to personal growth yet mindful of the need to be accepting, compassionate, patient, and grateful along the way. A strong sense of self-kindness allows you to acknowledge difficulties as a normal part of life, and to respect yourself as you progress on your self-love journey.

Since being kind to yourself includes how you tend to your needs, the benefits of self-kindness can help to improve your mental and physical health. Self-kindness is associated with happiness, optimism, curiosity, emotional intelligence, and well-being. Self-kindness can be helpful in reducing stress, anxiety, self-criticism, avoidance, and depression.

Take caution neglecting this seemingly simple but integral aspect of self-love.

You have already learned some helpful ways to practice self-kindness, such as practicing self-care (page 47), challenging negative thinking (page 86), and creating motivational messages (page 91).

Thinking about the definition of self-kindness, how are you nice to you?

NICE NOTES

Kindness includes generosity, helpfulness, tenderness, and consideration. Since being self-kind isn't always encouraged from a young age, sometimes it's easier to be kinder to others than to ourselves. However, self-love cannot develop without kindness. Therefore, it can be helpful to practice turning your kindness inward to foster this important aspect of self-love.

Now that you have gathered inspiration, it's time to practice self-kind statements. A simple way to show yourself kindness is by being supportive and encouraging (see Motivational Messages on page 91). Use the space below to help you craft thoughtful messages.

To continue this act of self-kindness, you may choose to transfer these messages onto small pieces of paper. If you wish to be reminded often, maybe you will choose a sticky note to be placed where you can see it repeatedly, such as above your desk, on your mirror, or on your closet door. If you choose to have a kind reminder every now and again, place it where you will see it infrequently, such as inside a notebook or at the bottom of a drawer, perhaps when you need your kindness the most.

BODY-KINDNESS

A healthy connection with your body influences self-love. Oftentimes people get distracted by things they do not like about their bodies. Sometimes this distraction becomes common and even obsessive. Developing an unhealthy relationship with your body is associated with anxiety, depression, self-harm, and risky behaviors.

Sometimes people fall into the trap of comparing their body to others, which causes them to be more dissatisfied with their body image. This is particularly dangerous when it comes to social media. Someone could find themselves comparing themselves to an idealistic image that is actually edited. Comparing yourself to distorted views of reality causes a vicious cycle of discontent.

An unhealthy relationship with our bodies causes us to disconnect from them, and we lose the ability to be grateful for what they offer us. Your body keeps you alive. It sends you messages that can be key to survival, such as when you are hungry, cold, experiencing aches, or are scared. Without body-kindness you risk fraying this connection, and that could be dangerous.

LISTEN TO YOUR HEART

Previously you were able to practice mindfulness (page 25). You learned to tune in to your breath and scan your body to find and release tension. Let's add on to that practice to help you attune to your body.

Find a comfortable seated position. Begin to focus on your breath. Try to breathe in and out through your nose. Notice the sensations in your body. Breathe in to the count of 1-2-3-4-5; breathe out to the count of 5-4-3-2-1. Notice the expansion and contraction of the chest. Scan for tension in the body. If you find any, allow your body to relax further on each exhale. Now, place your hands on your heart. Bring your awareness to the beating underneath your hands. Your heart is working to pump the vital source of oxygen through your body. As you continue to breathe, reflect on all that your heart has done for you. Your heart has fueled you every day. Take a moment to thank your heart for the love it has provided you.

How often do you connect to your body?

Have you stopped to thank your heart before?

What was it like to complete this practice?

Was it different from the previous mindfulness exercises?

This activity built upon your previous mindfulness strategies to focus on your heart. To continue developing a connection with your body you may choose to repeat this exercise as-is or you may opt to shift your focus to another body part.

SELFIE-LOVE

It's time to take a selfie! Do not change anything about your appearance prior to taking the photo. Give your selfie some love. Practice being kind to yourself by highlighting the things you like about you.

____

____

____

____

____

What are other details that you like about you that you cannot see in this photo?

____

____

____

____

MAKING HEALTHY CHOICES

By now, you've explored many ways to foster your self-care. You've explored strategies and developed a wellness plan (see page 58) to step into your power. Preventative strategies of self-love are another excellent way to be kind to yourself and build a strong foundation to protect yourself from harm.

As a teenager, you're capable of proactive, self-kind choices to take charge of your wellness. These include:

- Being mindful about eating. Quality nutrition provides you with the fuel you need to make the most out of every day.
- Spending time outdoors.
- Exercising to build strength. Regardless of your fitness level exercise can have a positive influence on your wellness.
- Getting quality rest.

- Avoiding drugs and alcohol. Alcohol affects your brain chemistry and drugs hinder your brain development.

Even small choices can be influential. Which of your health choices embody self-kindness?

What are some ways that you already make healthy choices?	What are some healthy choices you would like to make in the future?

THE BULLY VERSUS THE FRIEND

Your self-talk is the inner dialogue that you have with yourself (see My Inner Dialogue on page 82). Previously, you learned the impact of negative thoughts and the importance of transforming distorted thinking into healthy thoughts. Sometimes the process of challenging an unhelpful thought is easier said than done. We tend to have blind spots (see page 29) and obstacles that can make it harder to be kind to ourselves, even when we know that being nice to ourselves is the healthier, self-loving option.

Negative thoughts, unchecked, can link together to create a powerful inner voice. When this happens, your inner dialogue may be impulsive, aggressive, controlling, argumentative, and manipulative. Your internal tone shifts from being your encouraging friend to your very own bully. We think about bullies being other people, but it is particularly dangerous when you become your own bully.

Consider the characteristics of a bully. What are some things you may have said in the past to bully yourself? Before responding to this prompt, it may be helpful to consider your thoughts around the qualities you believe are negative (see My Personal Qualities, page 75).

___

___

___

___

If you heard someone saying such things to your friend, how would you respond?

If your loved ones heard someone saying such things to you, how would they respond?

In order to transform your inner tone from bullying to friendly, what promise do you need to make to yourself?

In order to maintain this promise, what feedback do you need to give yourself about your inner tone?

What do you need more of?

What do you need less of?

When you don't monitor your inner bully, it becomes stronger. It can become manipulative and sneaky. It can be helpful to pay attention to the quality of your self-talk to discern if the message is from your inner friend or inner bully. Think of your mind as a small stage with only one microphone. Your self-talk can be positive or negative, and when your friend and bully are fighting for control of the microphone your self-statements may be a bit mixed. Take control of who you let on your stage. When you catch yourself, curiously ask, "Who has the microphone?"

ROOM FOR GROWTH

Highlighting your strengths is a self-loving practice that can improve your self-esteem. With that being said, it is also important to recognize where there is room for growth. Typically we see these as negative qualities or weaknesses, but the truth is that these areas give us opportunities for personal growth.

Place a star next to all of the traits below that you believe represent an area of strength. Circle the traits in which you believe you have room for improvement.

Active	Hopeful	Secure
Adventurous	Independent	Sensitive
Affectionate	Observant	Serious
Alert	Open-minded	Silly
Amicable	Passionate	Sincere
Attentive	Patient	Spontaneous
Brave	Perceptive	Straightforward
Calm	Personable	Thankful
Charitable	Practical	Thorough
Compassionate	Prudent	Tidy
Cooperative	Punctual	Tolerant
Empathetic	Purposeful	Trustworthy
Gentle	Quiet	Warm
Helpful	Reflective	Wise
Honest	Romantic	Witty

Take a moment to brainstorm where you have opportunities to grow and list them in the box below. You can use the qualities circled on the previous page. For example, if you circled hopeful, you may specify "I would like to be more hopeful about my future career."

You may also find it helpful to review the traits you previously listed (see Positive, Negative, or Neutral on page 75). As you brainstorm, bear in mind that your opportunities may span beyond personality (e.g., I have room for growth in my time-management skills).

Opportunities for growth

Don't be so distracted with your opportunities for growth that you lose yourself in the process. Remember that you are worthy just as you are. Also, while you have areas you can courageously work to improve, keep the areas you already have as strengths in mind.

Think about the traits that you starred on page 105 . How can those strengths be used to help you with your opportunities to grow?

THE GRACIOUS GAP

Self-kindness is the practice of recognizing your capacity for growth yet being gracious to yourself as you fill that gap. While you may be excited about the destination, the ride should also be pleasant.

While you may not be where you wish, do not ignore your progress. For example, you may say to yourself, "I have room for growth in my leadership skills." Having room for growth doesn't mean you have not already improved. After thinking a bit more you may realize, "Although I can improve, I did sign up to run for vice president of my class. I am also trying to be more assertive, as I recognize my words are valuable. Although I have room for growth in this area, a positive quality is that I want to make sure that everyone is heard and is cooperative."

FILLING IN THE GAP

Choose four of the opportunities you listed in the Room for Growth exercise and practice graciously filling the gap with positive, kind self-talk.

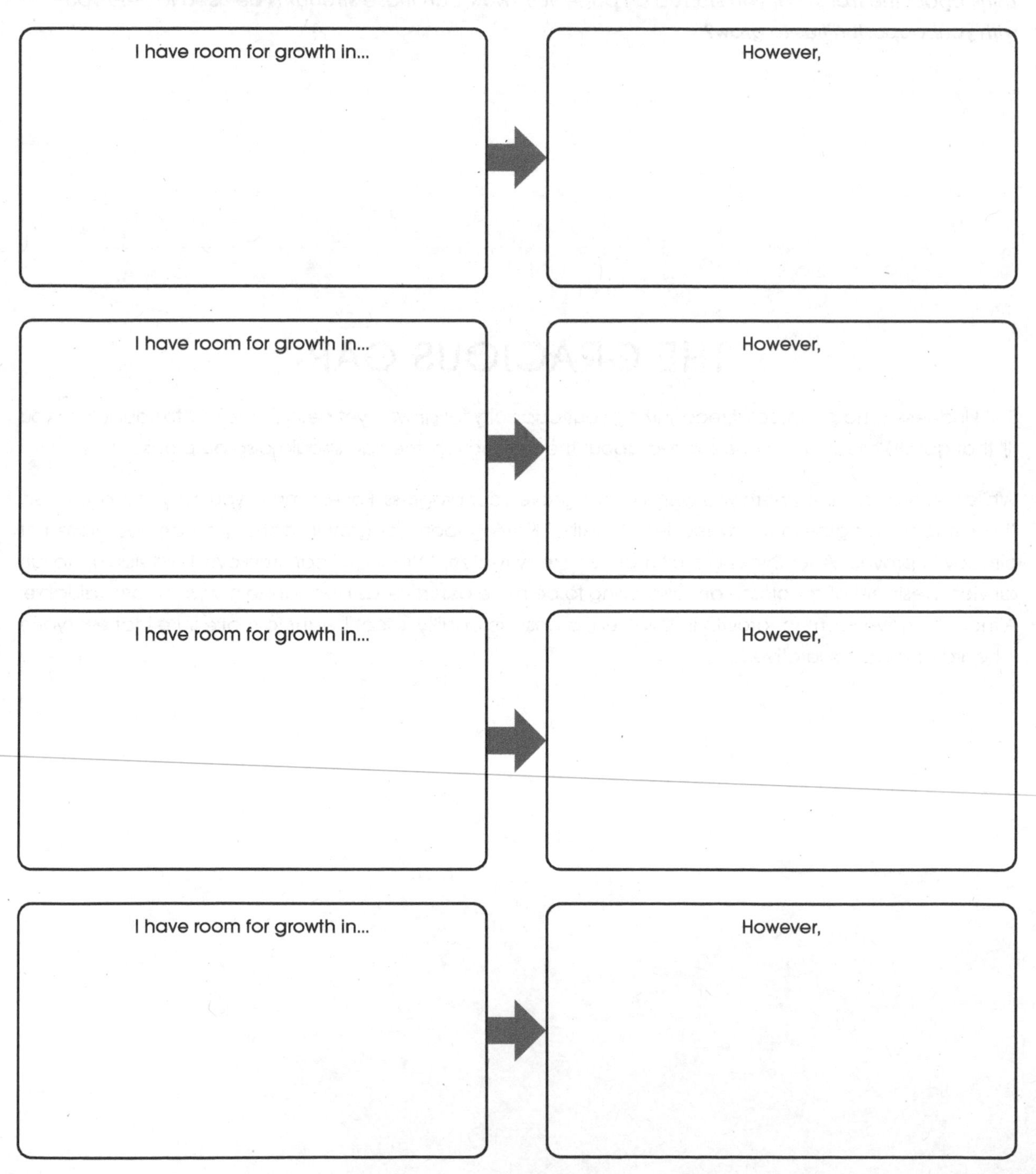

SETBACK SLINGSHOT

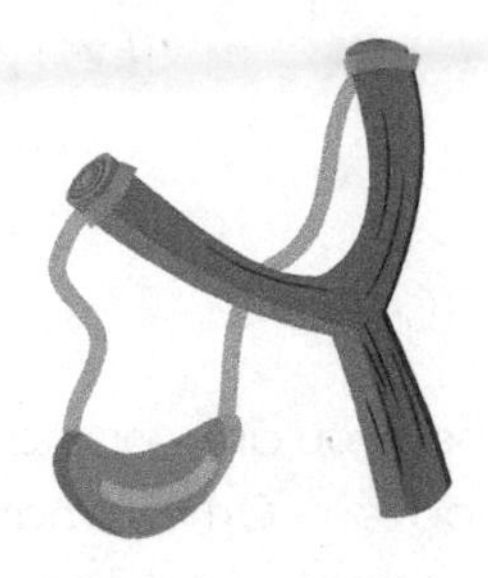

Setbacks are an inevitable part of life. No matter who you are or where you're from, you can't escape a setback at one point or another. Like a dance, we move through our journey trying our best to move forward; however, sidesteps and backsteps are to be expected. When this happens we tend to get self-critical, judgmental, and mean to ourselves. We could really benefit from being understanding, compassionate, and kind instead. Setbacks can provide us with a broadened perspective, and sometimes a learned lesson. Choosing to acknowledge and understand our setbacks can help us feel empowered and could provide us with the energy to move forward in our path again.

Think of a time that you experienced a setback and you criticized yourself. How could you have responded in a kinder way?

Use the prompts in the box to help you with this reflection.

I believe that...

I learned that...

This may have happened because...

I take full responsibility for...

I tend to...

Next time I can...

I didn't have control over...

From this experience...

In the future I hope to...

SELF-PATIENCE

"Every great dream begins with a dreamer. Always remember, you have within you the strength, the patience, and the passion to reach for the stars to change the world."

—Harriet Tubman

When you are working hard on your self-love, it is understandable to become impatient. On one hand, the eagerness can help to keep you focused on your goal of self-growth. On the other hand, you can become frustrated when your process doesn't happen as fast as you wish. As your aggravation increases, your motivation may diminish. Rushing toward a finish line may cause you to lose sight of your purpose. Patience allows you to be kind to yourself in your process. Reflect on your Mission Statement on page 40 as you contemplate ways to practice patience below.

In what areas could you benefit from being more patient?

____

____

What helps you to be more patient?

____

____

What are the signs that you are becoming impatient?

____

____

What can you do if you notice yourself becoming impatient?

____

____

EMBRACING IMPERFECTION

Nothing is perfect; no one is perfect. Aiming for an impossible standard can trick you into believing that you are failing when, in reality, you could be making wonderful progress. In contrast, practicing self-kindness can help to keep you from falling into the habit of striving for perfection and protect you against the consequences.

To practice embracing imperfection, consider the domains of your wellness. See page 50, Your Wellness Domains.

Select one of your wellness domains and write that label on the line below:

To practice shunning perfectionism you may simply choose to draw a line over, scribble over, or block out the word below:

PERFECT

Take a moment to visualize yourself achieving wellness in your selected area. What does a hopeful, yet realistic, standard of this aspect of your wellness look like? Use the space below to reflect. Feel free to explore with doodles or describe with words.

SELF-ACCEPTANCE

Self-acceptance is a process in which you acknowledge and embrace both your strengths and weaknesses. It is personal and realistic. Self-acceptance can help to shield you from self-judgment and release you from things you cannot control. Practicing self-acceptance can be a helpful way to be kinder to yourself. For example, self-acceptance can help you fill the gracious gap (page 107), recover from setbacks (page 109), and release perfection (page 111).

"A man cannot be comfortable without his own approval."

—Mark Twain

In the first box, describe a negative trait you may have. See Positive, Negative, or Neutral (page 75). In the second box, practice a counter that embodies self-acceptance.

In the first box, describe an area in which you have room for growth: See page 105, Room for Growth. In the second box, practice a counter that embodies self-acceptance.

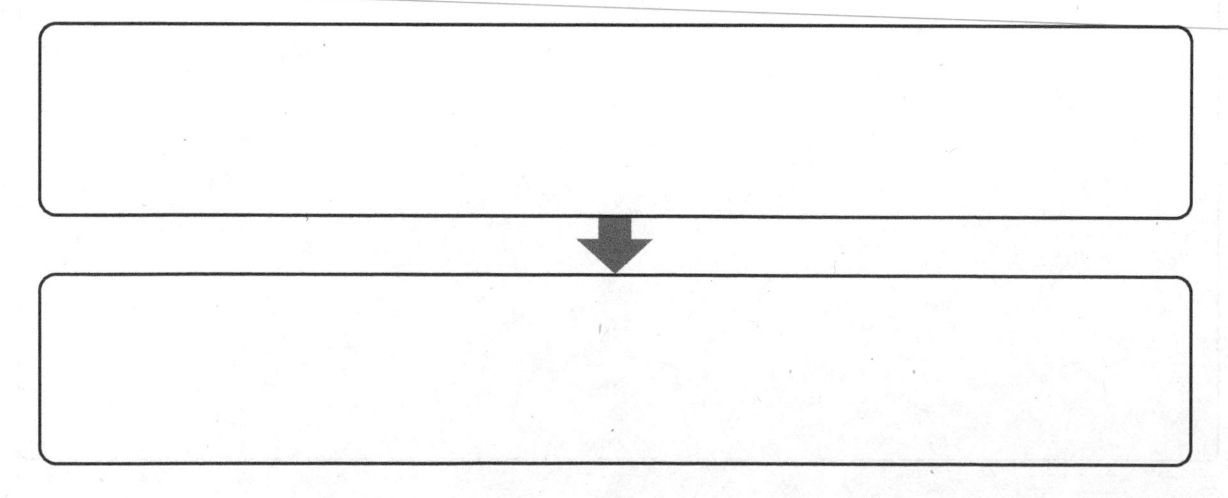

In the first box, describe a goal you have been striving toward for a long time. See page 163, Short-Term and Long-Term Goals. In the second box, practice a counter that embodies self-acceptance. You might want to jump back to this after reading the Self-Growth chapter (page 152) if you are having a hard time selecting a goal.

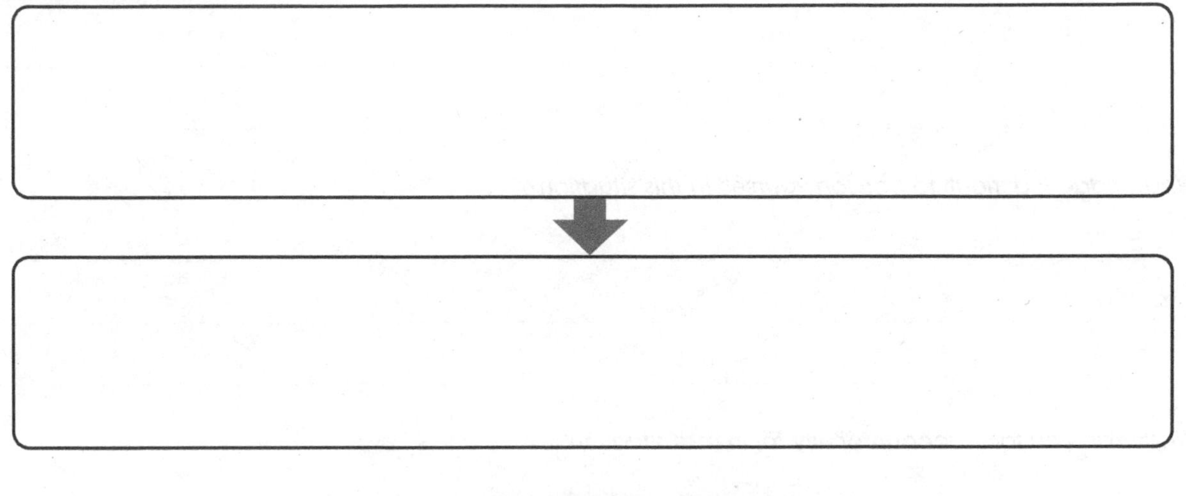

SELF-FORGIVENESS

"Don't let yesterday take up too much of today."

—Will Rogers

Forgiveness is a powerful tool in self-acceptance. When you choose to let go of a past negative occurrence, forgiveness is essential. It is not to be confused with excusing, condoning, minimizing, or ignoring. Instead, as a self-loving act, seeking forgiveness allows you to learn from your previous experiences, accept responsibility, take accountability, and set your intentions to learn and grow in the future.

Self-forgiveness can be a particularly difficult process since both the forgiver and forgivee lies within you. While it is empowering to have the power on both ends, it can also be complicated and requires a great deal of self-awareness and self-kindness to arrive at your personal reconciliation.

Avoiding self-forgiveness comes with consequences. The inability to forgive yourself has been associated with anxiety, depression, and a weakened immune system. On the other hand, choosing to forgive yourself can decrease the negative effects of guilt, demonstrate your respect for yourself, and allow you to foster your growth.

PRACTICING SELF-FORGIVENESS

Think of a time you struggled to forgive yourself.

What made it difficult to pardon yourself in this situation?

What can you take accountability for in that situation?

What was beyond your control in that situation?

What do you need to do in order to begin to let this go?

What lesson have you learned?

How does this example of forgiveness relate to your self-love practice?

Using the answers above, try this:

I forgive myself for (situation). I know that I was (accountability statement). I forgive myself because (self-love statement). In the future, (lesson learned).

Example: *I forgive myself for not showing up to soccer practice. I know that I was feeling a bit lazy and could have used the extra preparation. I forgive myself because I was able to listen to my body and I was exhausted. In the future, I will try to get better sleep the night before I should be playing so I don't have to let myself and my team down.*

I forgive myself for

I know that I was

I forgive myself because

____

____

____

In the future

____

____

____

GIFTS OF GRATITUDE

Practicing gratitude can be a practical tool of self-kindness. It begins from within by highlighting something you appreciate about yourself. The kindness evoked from gratitude can expand outward as well. For example, you may wish to acknowledge someone who has been caring to you or the community that you live in.

Each bit of gratitude is a gift. Draw a gift to represent someone or something that you are grateful for. Begin with self-kindness by depicting presents you have given yourself. Then feel free to expand into gifts you have been given and wish to give as well.

SELF-KINDNESS CHAPTER REFLECTION

CHAPTER 7

SELF-RESPECT

As a basic human right, everyone deserves respect. Being equal to others, you deserve respect from others and from yourself as well. While respecting others is honorable, habitually prioritizing their needs above your own is not self-loving. In addition, ignoring your needs for the sake of others can cause you to become stressed or unhappy.

Self-respect is an important virtue that includes your awareness of your worth, your ability to honor yourself, and your efforts to maintain your dignity. Self-respect is related to other essential aspects of self-love, such as self-esteem and self-acceptance. A sign that someone lacks self-respect is self-deprecation, or being critical about themself in a way that signifies a lack of peace within.

On the other side of the spectrum, it is important to note that self-respect is not to be confused with aggressiveness or entitlement. When this develops it is because someone deems him- or herself as more important than another person. Sincere self-respect humbly asserts that you are as worthy as anyone else. Therefore, the respect you deserve is neither more or less than that of anyone else, but it is essential nevertheless.

A strong sense of self-respect helps you to better respect others and to be better respected by others. Having dignity in your identity allows you to set an example, particularly in terms of how you wish to be treated. It also allows you to protect yourself with boundaries that may open to permit you to connect with others and close to protect you from harm.

With self-respect you recognize that you are priceless and cannot be objectified. You have a keen awareness of your personal values, which serves as an internal compass for the path you wish to walk in your life journey and provides the structure for you to build your identity. With all of that being said, honing your self-respect is a subjective experience that takes time to understand and implement. As you embark on this chapter of your journey, be sure to reflect on your unique identity and practice patience in the process.

Use the space below to brainstorm what you respect about yourself.

You may find inspiration from past activities such as My Self-Efficacy (page 80) and Nice Notes (page 98).

VALUES

In order to respect yourself, you have to know what you believe in and how you wish to represent yourself. Explore your values. Take a moment to reflect on who you are and who you wish to be. Several of the values below may apply to you, some perhaps more strongly than others. Those that match strongly with who you are can help to define your core values and support your self-respect.

Your values are embedded in your sense of purpose. Earlier, you created a Mission Statement (see page 40) to help you define your purpose. It may be helpful to revisit that statement to help you reconnect with your values.

1. ***For each value, place a + if you agree it is important to you or a—if it is not.***

2. ***To show the intensity, place up to three symbols. For example, if ambition is very important you may wish to put +++.***

3. ***As you place the corresponding symbols, think about the reason behind the value.***

Examples:

1. Achievement is important (++) to me. I believe that being able to succeed in my classes sets me up for a good future, but it is not the most important goal in my life. I know that weighing achievement above other values can lead to perfectionism, which is unhelpful for self-love.

2. Eccentricity is not really important to me at all (–). I do believe it is important to be my true self and I respect uniqueness, but I don't personally believe that this means I have to be eccentric to be who I am.

You can use the empty lines to add in additional values that may apply to you.

_____ Achievement
_____ Altruism
_____ Ambition
_____ Awareness
_____ Balance
_____ Beauty
_____ Charity
_____ Cleanliness
_____ Comfort
_____ Communication
_____ Connection
_____ Courage
_____ Dedication
_____ Eccentricity
_____ Fame
_____ Flexibility
_____ Freedom
_____ Fun
_____ Generosity

_____ Happiness
_____ Health
_____ Honesty
_____ Humility
_____ Humor
_____ Learning
_____ Logic
_____ Love
_____ Neutrality
_____ Originality
_____ Peace
_____ Politeness
_____ Practicality
_____ Productivity
_____ Prosperity
_____ Quality
_____ Recreation
_____ Reflection
_____ Respect

_____ Restraint
_____ Science
_____ Security
_____ Selflessness
_____ Sincerity
_____ Solitude
_____ Spirituality
_____ Stability
_____ Teamwork
_____ Traditionalism
_____ Versatility
_____ Wealth
_____ ____________________
_____ ____________________
_____ ____________________
_____ ____________________
_____ ____________________
_____ ____________________
_____ ____________________

CORE VALUES

When you refine your values, you prioritize what matters the most to you. In this process, you learn more about yourself. The better you know your true self, the more you know your preferences, needs, limitations, and aspirations.

Take a moment to review the values that you marked as important and place them in the corresponding boxes below.

+	++	+++

As you look at the domains you have created to prioritize your values, are there any you would move? If so, take a moment to place them in the appropriate section.

While all of the morals listed in the chart above are important to you, it is likely that those listed in the right column are your core values. These qualities combine to encompass who you are and who you wish to be. Knowing your core values is helpful because it helps you to realign with your true self. Core values help you to make decisions and prioritize your self-love.

From this section, choose your top five values that convey who you are as a person, what you believe in, and what you wish to embody in your life. The prompts on the next page will help you delve further into the connection that you have with each value.

Core value: ______________________________

This is important to me because...

____

____

Without this value...

____

____

I uphold this value by...

____

____

Core value: ______________________________

This is important to me because...

____

____

Without this value...

____

____

I uphold this value by...

____

____

Core value: ____

This is important to me because...

Without this value...

I uphold this value by...

Core value: ____

This is important to me because...

Without this value...

I uphold this value by...

Core value: ____

This is important to me because...

Without this value...

I uphold this value by...

CONGRUENCE

When there's consistency between what you believe in and how you behave, life tends to be easier and you tend to feel happier. On the other hand, when living a life that is misaligned with your values may cause you to experience an inner conflict (See Inner Conflict, page 43). When you are experiencing such internal friction, you are likely to develop negative feelings such as sadness, frustration, and resentment. For example, if one of your core values is honesty yet you cheated on an exam, your incongruence may prompt negative sentiments such as guilt and regret.

Think of a time when your behavior aligned with your values. Summarize that instance below:

Explain how being congruent in that moment affected you. If you get stuck, you may find it helpful to revisit your emotional exploration skills on page 19.

Think of a time when your behavior did not align with your values. Summarize that instance below:

Explain what hindered your ability to achieve congruence at that time.

Explain how this congruence affected you.

HONORING MY VALUES

"How you love yourself is how you teach others to love you."

—Rupi Kaur

Your core values give you an opportunity to honor your worth. Core values serve as guidelines for your self-respect and allow you to make informed rules to help you live an empowered, self-loving life. These rules keep you aware of how you treat yourself, how to treat others, and how you wish to be treated. Provide specific examples of how you will be congruent with each of your core values.

Example:

Core Value: Patience

When making a big decision, I will journal about my choices first.

When I find myself becoming impatient I will use mindfulness.

I will not act impulsively.

Place one of your core values into each shape below. Reflect on your present status for each. Have you recently been behaving in a manner that is consistent with this core value? If so, draw an equivalent shape and explain how you are achieving congruence. If not, draw a disproportionate shape and explain what is holding you back from achieving congruence.

"No one can make you feel inferior without your consent."

—Eleanor Roosevelt

Boundaries play an essential role in promoting and preserving self-respect. The mere decision to build boundaries is an act of self-love, since choosing to do so honors your worth and dignity. While this is a worthwhile task for everyone, the parameters to protect oneself tend to vary from person to person. As you reflect on your unique boundaries, it is important to devise strategies that will help you uphold your needs.

Boundary creation is an important start, but the work does not end there. Affirming your boundaries, particularly when they are tested, validates your sense of self-respect. In the process, it helps others acknowledge and respect you as well. Boundary management is an ongoing process in which you reevaluate your parameters and shift them as needed.

For example, you make take the time to reflect that certain comments, even joking in nature, are off limits and offensive for you. Imagine a friend calls you by a name that you find derogatory; however, your friend claims that it was all in jest and brushes it off without an apology. In this moment, it might be beneficial to step into your self-respect by highlighting your boundary, noting why it is important to you and asserting your limits. If this person is a true friend, they will be able to receive your feedback and honor this boundary in the future. On the other hand, if you notice that reminding your friend about a boundary has become a habit, this may be a signal to step back, reflect, and reassess.

It can be difficult to balance your needs with the temptation of self-sacrificing for the sake of others. From the first consideration that boundaries are needed to the times in which your limits are broached, managing boundaries can be a perplexing, yet purposeful, process. Considering the example above, imagine that your friend is going through a very difficult time in life. Being friends, you are aware that this person uses humor to keep serious topics light in order to cope. Knowing your friend is currently struggling, you might forsake the importance of asserting your boundary when your friend makes the insulting quip. However, the problem may persist over time. While you mean well to brush an insult under the rug for the sake of your friendship and your friend's emotional well-being, this may cause the problem to perpetuate, causing you to be hurt in the end.

INTRAPERSONAL BOUNDARIES

People often set boundaries for social situations; however, self-respect begins with how you treat yourself. Since you are responsible for your own behaviors, it is just as essential to formulate intrapersonal boundaries.

Your intrapersonal boundaries help you to regulate your reactions to your own prompts. The ability to be accountable for yourself by creating self-boundaries then helps to foster several self-loving domains, such as self-awareness, self-acceptance, self-care, and self-growth.

What are some examples of boundaries that you have for yourself?

What are some examples of intrapersonal boundaries you could benefit from creating?

What do you need to uphold your boundaries with yourself?

When was a time that you crossed a boundary of your own?

How did you notice that you crossed your own boundary?

What have you done to enhance this boundary since?

INTERPERSONAL BOUNDARIES

Interpersonal boundaries are the limitations set between yourself and others in order to foster mutual respect. You demonstrate respect for others by seeing and abiding by their interpersonal boundaries. You respect yourself by creating clear boundaries with others and enforcing them as needed.

What are some examples of interpersonal boundaries you currently have?

What is an example of a time in which you crossed someone's boundary?

How did you know you crossed a boundary?

What has changed since this event?

How do you know when someone has crossed your boundary?

What emotions arise when someone crosses one of your boundaries?

How do you react when someone crosses one of your boundaries?

How can you improve your boundaries with others?

THE MANY HATS WE WEAR

We all wear many hats in our lives. The boundaries you need and establish may vary from role to role. When we connect to who we are, including our personal mission and core values, it is possible for some boundaries to be a consistent thread in our hats. However, it is important to note that different situations and contexts may warrant a slight change in boundaries. This does not mean that you are being inconsistent with who you are; instead, it means that you are aware that context will vary throughout your life. It is unlikely you would wear a hard hat to a baseball game or a top hat to the beach. Matching roles and contexts help us to know what types of boundaries are appropriate.

MY HAT COLLECTION

Think about the different hats you wear. To start, there is a specific hat for the boundaries you have with yourself. It may be helpful to think about your overall cultural identity as well (see Cultural Exploration, page 42). Finally, your hats may also vary according to context. It is likely that your boundaries may differ between close loved ones, neighbors, colleagues, and strangers. Place your boundary domains in the column on the left. List the different roles you have in the top row. In each box, explore what that domain looks like within that role.

BOUNDARY DOMAINS	ROLES
Physical	**Student:** If I place my elbows out to the sides at school, no one should be within that space. **Child:** I like to hug my parents every day. When we are arguing I don't like to be touched at all. **Sibling:** When we were younger my brother and I would horseplay, but that's not an issue anymore. **Friend:** I love hugging my friends when I see them and when we say goodbye.

Example: *Building on the physical domain exemplified on the previous page, let's say the roles you have included are being a student, child, sibling, and friend. As a student you may find that your personal space at school is more distant than at home. You may also note whether you find it appropriate for someone at school to embrace you and how. As a child and sibling you may find that you are more comfortable with physical touch, yet you may still have your limits. As a friend you may clarify that you enjoy hugs when you greet and leave your friends. You may also specify that you do not find it appropriate for anyone in these contexts to be physically aggressive with you.*

BOUNDARY DOMAINS	ROLES

BOUNDARY RANGES

Boundaries tend to range from firm to flexible to open. Boundaries are most useful when the level of strength matches the situation. However, people tend to mistakenly match their boundaries to their personality or personal preference rather than considering the context. For example, you may see yourself as an easygoing person, but that does not mean that you have to neglect your self-respect by having permissive boundaries.

A firm boundary is like a building wall whereas an open boundary might be more like a line drawn in the sand, or perhaps no clear boundary at all. Think of a flexible boundary like a gate. With the flexibility of a gate you are able to choose when to protect yourself from outside forces, yet you may choose to open the doorway when the time is right.

Use the examples below to see if you can tell the difference between firm, flexible, and open boundaries. Read the case studies below and describe the type of boundaries Leona and Kyle have in the lines below.

Leona has been shy all of her life. As an introvert, she prefers to keep to herself. This preference has been evolving. For the past year she has found herself getting anxious in social situations, and recently she has little interest in leaving her home. When she experiences these worries she tends to keep them to herself. Although she hasn't spoken to anyone about her fears, she is worried that they are getting out of control and will affect her when she moves away for college next year.

Within the last few months, Kyle noticed a slow change beginning to happen with his friends. Originally, it seemed as if they were all making lighthearted jokes at one another, but over time, Kyla realized that he was bearing the brunt of the remarks. At first it was small and slight, he was even poking fun at his friends, so he didn't find it concerning. The intensity has grown and every time they get together, the odds are high that one of his friends will hit below the belt. Kyle usually enjoys spending time with his friends, but he's starting to question spending time with them.

Leona tends to have firm boundaries while Kyle appears to have open boundaries. However, both are facing consequences from being too far on either end and would benefit from improving their flexibility.

Review the chart below, and place a checkmark by each detail that relates to you. Be sure to consider your own view, as well as feedback that you have been given throughout your life.

FIRM	FLEXIBLE	OPEN
❑ Protect your personal information	❑ Be aware of who you are	❑ Easily share your personal information
❑ Avoid connection	❑ Value opinions of others	❑ Connect easily
❑ Rarely ask for help	❑ Consider feedback	❑ Value opinions of others over your own
❑ Detach	❑ Recognize when a boundary is crossed	❑ Tolerate disrespect
❑ Withdraw	❑ Know the need to shift boundaries in accordance with context	❑ Involve yourself in matters beyond yourself
❑ Isolate	❑ Respect yourself	❑ Prioritize others over yourself
❑ Reject others		

Are your boundaries generally more firm, flexible, or open?

____

____

____

____

What can you do to improve healthy boundaries?

____

____

____

____

BOUNDARY LEVELS

There are many variables to consider in order to create boundaries that uphold your self-respect. Your boundaries may vary by context, environment, and domain. For example, imagine Leona decides to see a counselor for her growing concerns. While her general preference may be to have firm boundaries, recognizing that it is in her best interest to be open and communicative, Leona may opt for more open or flexible boundaries in that context. For Kyle, he once had open and flexible boundaries with his friends because he was comfortable. While the people may seem the same, the changes may require him to shift his boundary level.

Using what you have learned, think about the different people in your life, including yourself and strangers.

Whom have you established mutual, healthy boundaries with?

Who has established clear boundaries with you but needs to learn your boundaries?

Whom have you established your own boundaries with but need to learn their boundaries in return?

Whom do you need to create boundaries with for the first time?

What do you need in order to establish helpful boundaries in the future?

YOUR REMOTE CONTROL

Active awareness will help you to recognize if your boundaries are being respected or disregarded.

To help you gauge, use your inner control system. When your boundaries are respected, you can continue to press play as usual. Sometimes, you need just a brief moment to pause. Other times, you may need to rewind in order to reflect and review the situation. There may also be times in which you need to stop altogether in order to remove yourself from the situation.

How do you know when to use each button?

Taking the time to pause, review, or rest are all acts of self-love. These are ways to give yourself a moment to remind yourself of your core values (see page 121), realign with them (refer to congruence on page 124), and proceed in a way that shows you respect yourself and want to be true to who you are.

What do you need when you're in a situation in which you need to pause?

What do you need when you're in a situation in which you need to stop?

ASSERTIVENESS

Assertiveness is a self-loving quality in which you recognize your worth and advocate for yourself. It is a skill that allows you to confidently and respectfully affirm your needs without being demanding or aggressive. You can improve your ability to be assertive over time, but it is helpful to begin this practice at a young age.

Assertiveness comes with many benefits. It is associated with improvements in mental health, happiness, self-esteem, autonomy, self-acceptance, and personal growth. The benefits of assertiveness are not limited to you, because assertiveness is not selfish. When you are assertive, the people you interact with are also fortunate to experience respectful and cooperative communication.

How can Leona practice assertiveness?

How can Kyle practice assertiveness?

Give an example of a time that you needed to practice assertiveness:

What qualities do you have that help you to be assertive?

What opportunities for growth do you have in terms of your assertiveness?

If these questions were a bit difficult, you might want to flip forward to Tips to Build Better Boundaries on page 140, and come back.

TESTING BOUNDARIES

To practice assertiveness, clearly communicating your boundaries with others is key. When people know your boundaries, they will be less likely to cross them. Assertiveness can be particularly helpful when you need to enforce your boundaries after they are crossed. Even when a boundary is crossed, assertiveness can help you to rebuild and improve for the future.

Think of a time when someone crossed your boundary. Place an X on the scale from passive to aggressive to represent how you reacted at that time.

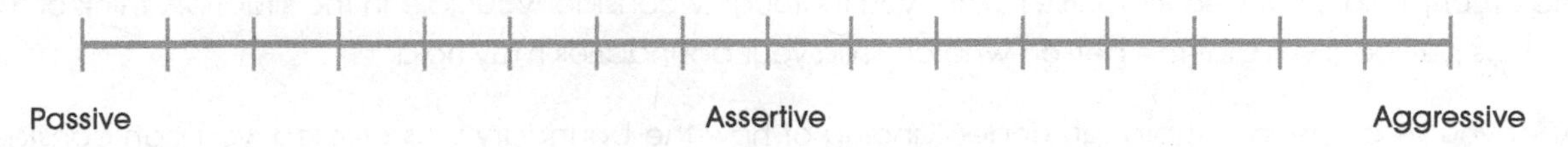

Place a star to represent how you would have liked to react at that time.

What was helpful in that situation?

Looking back, what could you have done to improve the situation?

TIPS TO BUILD BETTER BOUNDARIES

In a situation when your boundaries are tested, you have the opportunity to embody self-respect by choosing to improve your boundaries. It can be difficult to manage the careful balance between being passive and aggressive. The six simple tips below can help you to practice assertiveness.

1. Be prepared. When your boundaries are tested, it's important to avoid reacting impulsively. Take the time to pause and step back. Use this time to reflect on the situation and broaden your perspectives. Begin with self-exploration. Remember your worth, reconnect with your values, and remind yourself why your boundaries are important. Then, try to understand your role in the scenario. When you take the time to consider your responsibilities, you may come to realize that you forgot to make your boundary clear to the other person, but also to yourself. After you thoroughly consider your role in the situation, think of the various perspectives that the person who crossed your boundaries may hold.

After you've come to a thorough understanding of how the boundary was crossed, you can consider how to resolve the concern and move forward. Contemplate the void that needs to be filled. Finally, prepare yourself by deliberating how you can fill the void in an assertive way that upholds your self-respect while maintaining respect for the other person as well.

Example: *Jamil and Alana have been friends since they met in class a few years ago. Recently, they have been talking more and Jamil is now interested in being more than friends. After a lot of time just talking, he asked Alana to hang out after school on Friday. He has been looking forward to it all week and it seemed as though Alana was too. On Friday Jamil thought it was odd that he didn't hear from Alana. He sent her a few messages to follow up. Later that night Alana responded that she was sorry but something came up. Jamil was confused and this quickly grew into irritation. He had questions that he wanted answered and felt disrespected. How could Jamil prepare in this situation?*

____

____

____

2. Be clear. Your self-reflection from step 1 provides a foundation for your discussion. Your worth, values, and perspectives are what fuel you to address this potential misunderstanding. In order to clearly convey these important concepts, you must be concise and direct. It can be helpful to brainstorm what you plan to say by writing key components or practicing what you hope to say out loud. Be sure to use accurate information to avoid confusion. Although you may have a lot to say, try to pace yourself by providing essential components of your assertiveness in small bits to promote clarity understanding.

Example: *Jamil felt disrespected. He wants to share his perspective, but he is confused about why this bothers him so much. Put yourself in Jamil's shoes: What are some values that may have been affected and boundaries that may have been crossed in this scenario? How can Jamil clarify these for himself in order to convey them to Alana?*

____

____

____

3. Be respectful. Remember, discussing your boundaries is an interpersonal process. Although your self-respect is on the agenda, mutual respect is essential. As you convey your points, it is important to be kind, calm, attentive, and open in the process. If you do not embody these traits, it is likely that the assertiveness you wish to convey will be perceived as aggressiveness instead. Although you previously prepared by reflecting on the other person's possible perspective(s), in order to maintain balance, you must allow them the space to share their views as well. Try your best to maintain eye contact and convey your sincerity with a collected tone. Actively listen to what they share rather than using the time to selfishly gather your debate. Keep in mind that discussing a boundary that has been tested is not about right or wrong. Instead, it is a self-loving process in which you advocate for your growth and the growth of others around you.

Example: *In wanting to clarify what happened, Jamil is also curious about Alana's perspective. While his frustration is valid, her experience is relatively unknown. How can Jamil balance wanting to share his view while also being open to hearing Alana's?*

____

____

____

4. Be positive. It can be intimidating to take a stance for your boundaries. Nevertheless, it is a positive, self-loving act. Be optimistic that you have the power to influence the process and can maintain compassion for the person who crossed your boundaries along the way. With that in mind, release responsibility for how the person reacts and take accountability for how you present yourself. Be confident and grounded in your worth, purpose, and present intentions. Although the goal is a productive process resulting in improved boundaries, set your intention that regardless of the outcome, you can be proud that you demonstrated self-respect.

Example: *While Jamil wants to address the situation, he is also worried about overreacting. He is concerned that if he reacts too strongly he will not be true to himself and Alana will also lose interest in him. How can Jamil infuse positivity into his approach?*

____

____

____

5. Be flexible. Being assertive means protecting your boundaries without stubbornly ignoring the views of the other person. Ideally, both parties show respect, accountability, and responsibility. It is possible that the conversation can prompt you to notice where you could have contributed to the misunderstanding. It is also possible that the discussion may shine a light on a blind spot (see page 29) that you did not previously consider. Be flexible to the other person's needs and consider forgiveness to foster growth.

Example: *When discussing this situation with Alana, she shares that she had a family emergency come up and that took precedence. How can Jamil be flexible enough to honor her reality while still remaining true to his self-respect?*

____

____

____

6. Be persistent. In some instances, the person who tested your boundaries may continue to step over your limits. When this happens, it is important for you to be consistent, firm, and grounded in your self-respect. It is possible that you may need to escalate your intensity to appropriately reinforce your boundary, but this can be a tricky process. You do not want to allow someone to lure you to cross the line into aggressive behavior. You may need to seek help from others. Aid can be as simple as seeking advice; however, depending on the situation, you may need to seek professional help (e.g., police, mental health therapist, attorney).

Example: *Jamil comes to the conclusion that a family emergency is certainly an understandable reason to cancel; however, a simple message when Alana was alerted could have been helpful. Alana agrees, apologizes, and they make plans for the following Friday. If a similar concern were to repeat itself, how could Jamil address this situation?*

____

____

____

BOUNDARIES WITH BULLIES

From time to time, people may test your boundaries. When this happens, it provides an opportunity to assert your stance and uphold your self-respect. Bullies are a prime example of people who may push your boundaries. Previously you learned that a bully may be a part of your inner dialogue (see The Bully Versus the Friend on page 102), but this is not the only place a bully may be hidden. A bully can be sneaky and may be within your friend or family circles.

Three out of four students share they have been bullied in their lifetime. Bullies can be verbally or physically abusive. It can be really hard to embrace self-love when you are influenced by a bully. Being bullied has been associated with sleep issues, depression, self-harm, and suicide. Sometimes people assume that you will outgrow the influence of a bully, but this isn't necessarily true. For one, studies have shown that bullying is linked to depression in adulthood. In addition to this, bullies exist in adulthood as well.

Bullies often intentionally select people to harm whom they believe are vulnerable. You are not powerless when it comes to bullies. Instead of giving in to bullies, use these moments as an opportunity to embrace your self-respect. Since the presence and effects of bullying last well into adulthood, it is helpful to learn how to handle bullies now to have a solid, self-respecting method to utilize should this occur in the future.

Who has bullied you?

Describe your boundaries when you were bullied:

Knowing what you know now about assertiveness, healthy boundaries, and self-love, how would you like to address bullies in the future?

HEALTHY RELATIONSHIPS

Not all relationships pressure your boundaries; healthy relationships can help you enhance your self-respect. Positive people can help you to see your worth, even in times that you may not. They can assist you in creating your boundaries, and they can also show you that your boundaries can be acknowledged. On top of this, when you are having trouble forming or enforcing your limits, you can look to those with whom you have healthy relationships as examples of connections based on respect, care, and love.

In the box below, place the initials of the people with whom you believe you have healthy relationships.

Below are several qualities that are commonly found in healthy relationships. Place a star by each quality you believe is important to you. You can use the blank spaces to add additional qualities that are meaningful to you. Place the initials from the previous page next to each corresponding characteristic.

Consideration	Kindness	Care
Trust	Support	Autonomy
Individuality	Understanding	Compromise
Engagement	Effort	Honesty
Respect	Fun	Communication
Equality	Connection	Compassion

What qualities are important to you in a healthy relationship?

____

____

____

____

Considering the relationships you listed in the box above and the qualities that are important to you in a healthy relationship, what are you missing from your relationships?

____

____

____

____

How can you improve your relationships?

IMPROVING MY SUPPORT SYSTEM

"Surround yourself with only people who are going to lift you higher."

—Oprah Winfrey

The relationships you have combine to create your support system. This can include the connections you have at home, school, in community groups, or even online. Having healthy relationships in your support system can help you to embrace and uphold your self-respect. A positive sense of support can help to decrease your distress, protect you in tough times, and improve your overall quality of life. Your support system begins from the time you are born and although it will likely change throughout your lifetime, its importance remains the same.

REFLECTING ON YOUR SUPPORT SYSTEM

Take a moment to consider the domains of your personal wellness (see page 50). Do you have healthy relationships to foster each segment?

1. Place your name in the circle on the next page. Use the spokes to represent each of your wellness domains. Create additional lines as needed. From each branch, place the names of the people who presently provide support (see Exploring My Support System on page 68) for that aspect of your wellness and help you to maintain balance.

2. Next, consider if there is someone with whom you have a healthy relationship that you have not previously considered to be a part of your support system. Could this person help inspire or encourage you to fulfill any of your wellness domains? If so, place their name with a question mark in the corresponding area.

3. Finally, consider anyone who is unsupportive in your life; specifically, someone who is a poor influence on your wellness. Place that person's name in the corresponding area with a strike-through line over it.

Example

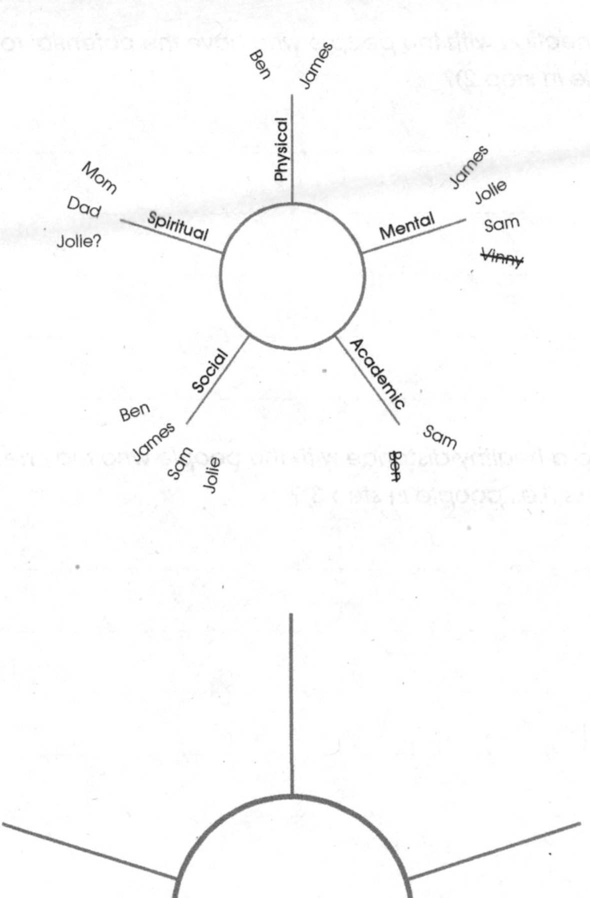

How can you maintain a healthy relationship with the people who positively impact your support system?

How can you foster a connection with the people who have the potential to positively influence your support system (i.e., people in step 2)?

What can you do to create a healthy distance with the people who may negatively influence at least one aspect of your wellness (i.e., people in step 3)?

FORGIVENESS

"The only thing evil can't stand is forgiveness."

—Fred Rogers

The struggle to forgive is a common obstacle in self-kindness. Believing that you have done something wrong can keep you stuck in the past. This may include things that you regret saying or doing, as well as things you regret not saying or doing. These obstacles can cause you to feel ashamed. In order to move forward, you must learn the process of forgiveness. Forgiveness is not to be confused with condoning, ignoring, minimizing, or supporting, but simply a promise to learn and grow.

Previously, you explored the importance of Self-Forgiveness (see page 113) in order to improve your self-kindness. However, forgiveness is often an interpersonal process in which you need to apologize or bestow forgiveness to others in order to move on.

APOLOGIES

An apology can be a powerful catalyst to humbly seeking genuine forgiveness. In a genuine apology you take accountability and share your plans for improvement. Reflect on apologies you may need to provide to others in order to move forward. Place those examples in the box below.

Choose an example from above and follow the prompts below.

I am sorry that...

I own that I...

In the future I plan to...

I hope...

Reflect on apologies you have waited for, that have caused you to be tethered to the past. Place these examples in the box below.

Although it may be easier to let go when someone offers you an apology, you are able to release the rope on your own. When you are dependent on an apology in order to move forward you give that person the rope, and they hold a sense of power in your life that they may not have earned. Being tethered can weigh you down and hold you back from growth. Instead of desperately waiting for the apology you are owed, you can make the active choice to move forward by letting go of the rope on your own accord. Even without that individual seeking forgiveness, you can progress by using your self-awareness, reflecting on learned lessons, and living a life that aligns with your mission.

How can you let go of seeking an apology for any of the items in the box above?

SELF-RESPECT CHAPTER REFLECTION

CHAPTER 8

SELF-GROWTH

Change is inevitable. Over time, you change, and the world around you transforms as well. As you adapt to these changes, it is a self-loving decision to embrace the process of growth. There's no such thing as perfection and no particular standard of growth that you need to achieve. Rather, the reality is that growth is never truly complete.

Acknowledging this truth can open your mind to the vast potential you have to grow. When you accept that there isn't a finish line, self-love becomes an exciting adventure in which you are continually seeking opportunities to learn, love, and thrive. Rather than obsessing about becoming captain of your sports team or valedictorian of your graduating class, you infuse self-love in each step you take toward your aspiration, which allows you to enjoy the journey along the way. It is a self-loving practice to recognize where you may have an opportunity to learn, improve, and strive to be the best version of you that you can be.

Within the overall process of self-growth, you seek to understand your blind spots (see page 29), welcome opportunities for growth (see page 105), and achieve congruence between your ideal self and your true self (see Exploring Inner Conflict, page 44; Congruence, page 124; and Honoring My Values, page 125). You become aware of obstacles that may hinder your progression (see Obstacles in Self-Love on page 11) and the methods you take to triumph over those hurdles. Even in times in which you experience a setback, self-growth also includes the power you evoke to propel yourself forward once again (see Setback Slingshot, page 109).

Counseling psychologist Dr. Kenneth Nowack highlights that initiating new behaviors is often difficult. It can be challenging to turn your goals on paper to actionable achievements. Instead of solely focusing on goal-setting, you may find it beneficial to shift to a goal-flourishing mindset. The self-loving process of goal-flourishing includes reflection, highlighting strengths, identifying goals, fostering motivation and encouragement, social support, relapse prevention, and evaluation This empowerment method allows you to create a thorough plan with a realistic overview of your aspirations, methods to support change, and strategies to account for setbacks along the way. In order to benefit from the self-loving process of self-growth, awareness, kindness, and respect are needed along the way.

THE PERFECT PEPPERED MOTH

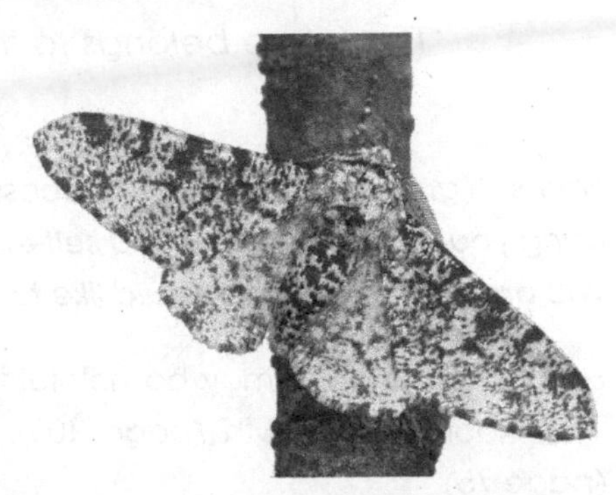

Historically, the peppered moth had a pale, speckled appearance. Since the coloring matched the growth typically found on tree bark, it provided excellent camouflage. Due to the Industrial Revolution, the soot levels rose in the area, and the moth's coloration was no longer a source of strength. Around 1819, a genetic mutation caused a black variant of moth, which blended in well and started to thrive in these conditions. As clean air legislation became enacted, a resurgence in the original peppered variety was seen.

Neither variety is perfect. Under different circumstances, one would survive more easily than another. If the mutation never occurred, perhaps the species would have been threatened by extinction. While at one time the lighter moth may have seemed adaptive, at another the darker moth would be noted as better suited for survival.

What does the history of the peppered moth tell you about change?

HOPES AND DREAMS

"The future belongs to those who believe in the beauty of their dreams."

—Franklin D. Roosevelt

Your self-growth is a personal process. To begin, it can be helpful to connect with who you are by using your self-awareness and self-exploration. While connecting with your true self, consider where you are and where you would like to be. What are your hopes and dreams for the future?

For this reflection, it may be helpful to jump back to My Mission Statement (page 40), Values (page 119), Room for Growth (page 105), The Gracious Gap (page 107), and/or My Personal Qualities (page 75).

VISUALIZATION

In addition to thinking about where you wish to be in the future, it's empowering to visualize this happening. For example, instead of merely thinking, one day I would like to buy a car, take it one step further by envisioning what this would look like. In this given scenario, what would it look like leading up to owning a car of your very own? What does the car of your dreams look like? What would it be like on the day you purchase the car?

Choose one of your future dreams. Set a timer for one minute. Close your eyes and allow yourself to immerse in that given visual.

When your time is up, use the space below to reflect.

You can repeat this activity to help you take your brainstorming and empowerment to another level. When you continue, you may choose to further the same dream, or you may select a different aspiration. As you delve further, you may benefit from increasing the time allotted and depth of reflection as well.

VISION BOARD

One way to further your visualization is to create a vision board. This gives you an overall image and reminder of your aspirations. Images can inspire and help us to recognize elements that we cannot fully describe with words. Considering where you wish to be in your future, create a small vision board on the next page. Add images that align with your hopes and dreams (see page 154). You may choose to print pictures, create your own doodles, or both. Feel free to add powerful words or phrases that fit to formulate your future vision.

For this activity, music can help you to get into a creative zone. To get yourself in the zone, you may want to put on your favorite empowering songs to help infuse some inspiration while you work on your vision board.

What was it like to create your vision board?

What pieces from your vision board stand out for you?

When creating your board, did any negative thinking patterns arise? If so, note them here and practice challenging those negative thoughts.

Consider the concept of congruence (see page 124). Does your vision board align with your core values?

What strengths do you have to achieve the hopes and dreams encapsulated on your board?

Considering your vision board, where do you believe you have room for growth?

Provide some examples of positive self-talk statements (e.g., affirmations, motivational messages) that you can use to practice self-kindness as you create your vision board.

SETTING SELF-LOVING GOALS

Setting goals can seem intimidating. However, when you infuse your goals with self-love, it can be an enjoyable process. The key difference pertains to your perspective in the process. Without self-love, you may set goals without reflecting on what's important to you. You may veer off into a path that doesn't truly align with who you are, and investing your time and energy into it can be particularly draining. Over time you can lose sight of the goal at hand and can become discouraged.

On the other hand, when you embed self-love you conscientiously create goals that are congruent with who you are and, hence, are naturally motivated and believe in your ability to achieve your aspirations. When setting self-loving goals, happiness is not a destination, but an experience. The journey to goal-attainment is just as important as achieving the goal itself. You craft considerate plans to achieve each aim, including critical steps along the way, support to aid in your progress, and strategies to face your obstacles.

Think about how you have set goals in the past.

What self-loving elements have you included in previous goal processes?

What self-loving elements do you intend to include in your future goal processes?

CAREER PLANNING

At this point in your life, you're likely thinking about your career aspirations. It can seem daunting to select a path that is unfamiliar to you. While you may not know about the field, do not minimize what you know about you. To begin to clear a path, consider your experiences, skills, strengths, likes, and dislikes. This self-exploration can help you begin to visualize the future of your dreams.

The chart below will help you to begin to form a career path. A few examples are provided; however, fill in the first column with other occupations that may appeal to you. In the second column, note what parts of that position are appealing to you and align with your strengths, skills, experiences, and preferences. In the third column, highlight the aspects of that career that may not be congruent with who you are. Finally, any questions that arise in the process in the last column. Seek the answers by researching the occupation, interviewing professionals, and maybe exploring the field through a shadowing opportunity.

PROFESSION	PROS	CONS	QUESTIONS
Engineer			
Nurse			
Entrepreneur			
Teacher			

PROFESSION	PROS	CONS	QUESTIONS

SMART GOALS

"It does not do to dwell on dreams and forget to live."

—Albus Dumbledore

Uncertainty pertaining to goals can cause psychological distress. Researchers at the University of Liverpool found that people who are depressed create goals differently. The difference is not that they create fewer goals; instead, their goals tend to be more abstract. When you're setting goals, take adequate time to perform a thorough evaluation, establish concrete goals, and clarify how they can be achieved. In order to do so, it can be helpful to assure that your goals are SMART.

Specific: Does your goal have precise details?

Measurable: Do you have clear methods to help you track progress?

Attainable: Is it plausible for you to achieve this goal?

Relevant: Does your goal connect to who you are?

Timely: Does the goal have a realistic and flexible timeline?

Example: *For the next month, I will use my gratitude journal at least once per day for at least five days per week.*

In the boxes below, explain how each SMART segment is achieved for the given example.

GOAL	S	M	A	R	T
1					
2					

GOAL	S	M	A	R	T
3					
4					

CREATE SMART GOALS

In your self-love journey thus far you have had many opportunities to reflect on potential personal growth goals. Now, you will have the opportunity to transform those hopes and dreams into SMART goals. To begin, practice creating SMART goals based on your wellness domains and aspirations. Reflect on the gap between your current wellness (see page 51) and your desired wellness. Consider the plans you created to promote self-love (see My Wellness Plan on page 58). Use the template to help you create at least one goal per dimension. After creating your goal, use the checkboxes to make sure the goal is SMART. If you notice a section is missing, revise your goal as needed.

WELLNESS DOMAIN	GOAL	S	M	A	R	T

SHORT-TERM AND LONG-TERM GOALS

"You can't cross the sea merely by standing and staring at the water."

—Rabindranath Tagore

It is common to feel overwhelmed when brainstorming your long-term goals. The time between then and now gives you space to second-guess your dreams. Nevertheless, long-term goals are beneficial as they give you sufficient time to achieve your goal. Furthermore, if things do not go to plan, long-term goals allow you the flexibility to infuse self-loving practices such as patience and kindness to help you buffer your fall. Long-term goals can help you to highlight your future aspirations. Short-term goals can be crafted to help you achieve milestones along the way to making your long-term dreams come true. We tend to be more motivated to achieve short-term goals, as they seem more plausible. To find a balance, you can benefit from using a combination of both.

BRAINSTORM YOUR FUTURE ASPIRATIONS

Use the space below to brainstorm your future goals.

After brainstorming, create as many long-term personal growth goals as you'd like. Be sure to use the SMART format. Use the staircase strategy to create short-term building blocks in subsequent layers to help you achieve your dream. For example, if you want to complete a triathlon, you might choose to take a step each for swimming, riding, and running.

Long-Term Goal

Short-Term Goal 3

Short-Term Goal 2

Short-Term Goal 1

30-DAY SELF-LOVE CHALLENGE

The pursuit of self-growth is a healthy challenge. Planning and consistency are two key elements to help you along your journey. Creating a personalized challenge can help you to consider both short and long-term aspirations while creating healthy habits. For example, a 30-day challenge can include your mini-goals that combine to help you achieve your larger goal by the end of the 30 days. Say you would like to complete this workbook in 30 days, then perhaps you might want to aim to complete two chapters per week.

For this task, your SMART goal is to increase your self-love by practicing a self-loving task at least one time per day for 30 days.

Consider the seven segments of self-love (see page 16). Create small, actionable self-loving tasks, completing one per day.

30-DAY CHALLENGE

TIPS:

- Start small, beginning with tasks in which you have high self-efficacy.
- Try to increase the intensity as the challenge progresses.
- Include breaks as needed. After all, a part of self-love is patience and listening to your needs.
- Place this challenge somewhere you can see it, and practice accountability.

1	2	3	4	5
6	7	8	9	10
11	12	13	14	15
16	17	18	19	20
21	22	23	24	25
26	27	28	29	30

MY SELF-GROWTH MAP

Now that you have an idea of your future dreams and have clarified some short- and long-term goals, it's time to put it all together in a self-growth map. A self-growth map will help you to keep your goals in order. You will be able to consider what helps you to fuel your tank and what helps you in your journey. You will also be able to take a realistic look at the obstacles that you may face in your path, which gives you the opportunity to reconnect to your values and strategize accordingly.

1. Select one long-term personal growth goal.

2. Draw your path to your goal. Remember, straight paths are rather unlikely.

3. Include roadblocks and hurdles you may encounter (see Roadblocks to Self-Love, page 14), such as a closed road.

4. Include supports that may help you, such as signs of encouragement (see Encouragers, page 91).

5. Include premature exits that are likely to tempt you to detour from your goal.

SELF-GROWTH MAP REFLECTIONS

What goal have you selected?

How does this goal relate to your self-love journey?

Where are you presently with this goal?

How far have you come with this goal?

What roadblocks do you anticipate in your path?

How do you plan to handle your roadblocks?

What sources of support will you have in your path?

How will you know when to seek support?

How will you know when you are tempted to abandon your path?

How will you handle the times in which you are tempted to abandon your path?

HANDLING SETBACKS

"Life is like riding a bicycle. To keep your balance, you must keep moving."

—Albert Einstein

When you encounter a setback, you naturally begin to question your goal. You may begin to assess the pros and cons associated with the goal, and whether it is still important for you. Sometimes setbacks start a snowball effect. Rather than getting up, dusting off your hands, and moving forward, when affected by the disappointment of a setback, you may no longer see your goals as doable or desirable. Experiencing setbacks can be discouraging and may tempt you to forfeit your future aspirations.

Previously you learned about the likelihood of setbacks as you learn and grow, and the importance of practicing self-kindness as they occur. In addition, it is important to proactively consider your obstacles so you can equip yourself with the tools to handle them. Think about it this way, if you're planning a walk in the park, a 50 percent chance of rain could be a setback. However, this doesn't mean you can't enjoy your stroll. Perhaps you grab an umbrella or a raincoat to prepare for the rain and avoid the potential weather hurdle.

Planning ahead allows you the openness to monitor and adjust to feedback. A continued connection to your self-awareness may also help you to deter future setbacks. If you know that lack of sleep will cause you to be groggy at school, for example, then you can intentionally aim for a restful evening prior to a big exam the next morning.

In addition, continued setbacks in an area can be used as flags to reconsider your approach. If you realize that simply hopping into bed earlier doesn't equate to improved sleep, then over time, you may use methods to adjust your sleeping routine. Ultimately, you may learn that you achieve ample rest by using an evening meditation, turning off your devices, and making a gratitude list before bed.

What setbacks may you face in your path of self-growth?

How will you handle these setbacks?

What type of self-kindness statement could you use for your slingshot if this occurs? See page 109, Setback Slingshot.

THE HIDDEN GIFT IN CHALLENGES

"We may encounter many defeats but we must not be defeated."

—Maya Angelou

Challenges are opportunities for you to triumph. We often think about difficult times negatively; however, if you look close enough, a positive perspective will help you to highlight the silver lining. You may think the absence of a challenge in pursuit of your goals ideal, but according to positive psychologist Mihaly Csikszentmihályi, without challenge we may actually be quite apathetic and bored. When we are equipped for the difficult task at hand, we experience flow. Also referred to as being in the zone, flow is a positive mental state in which you enjoy, and are deeply immersed, in the difficult task at hand. With this in mind, a challenge can be a positive experience.

Revisit the activities you explored in My Self-Efficacy (page 80) and Setback Slingshot (page 109). Place those activities in the appropriate section below.

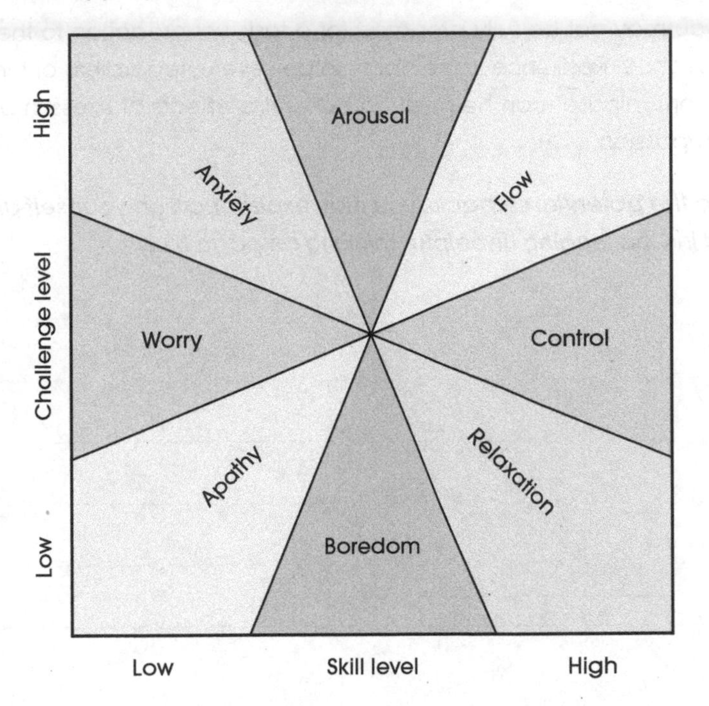

Consider your personal growth goals. What do you need in order to achieve flow while pursuing those goals?

APPLYING A SILVER LINING

Even in times when you may not be fully prepared for a task, your reaction to the challenge can show the positive trait of resilience. Resilience is the ability to persevere, regardless of hindrances and defeats along the way. A resilient mindset can help you to buffer the effects of stress in a challenging situation with the power of compassion.

Apply a silver lining to the potential setbacks you may experience on your self-growth journey. Use the skills you learned in Challenging Unhelpful Thinking on page 83.

____

____

____

____

____

____

LEARNED LESSONS

"I have not failed. I've just found 10,000 ways that won't work."

—Thomas A. Edison

Setbacks can be informative if you choose to empower yourself with learned lessons within them. Multiple unsuccessful attempts at a goal could mean that the method is flawed, the goal is not congruent with who you are, or many things in between. For example, you may notice that you have a bad habit of being late to your classes. Continually being late may be discouraging, and may have consequences to your success at school as well. You may set a goal pertaining to timeliness and still find yourself struggling. This doesn't mean that you can't achieve this goal over time; instead, this can be an opportunity to explore what is contributing to the problem in order to learn your lesson and create a plan for the future. From delving further you may find that you tend to chat with your friends for too long in between your classes or that stopping at your locker between every class is taking up too much time.

What lessons have you learned from pursuing personal goals in the past?

What lessons can you learn from your previous setbacks?

How will you infuse these learned lessons into your future aspirations?

MY SUPPORT SYSTEM

Your social support system (see page 68) can be a powerful resource in your self-growth process.

We are happier when we feel supported. In order to be supportive, the individuals in your life do not need to provide you direct help. Just having their encouragement as you walk your own path is beneficial.. As you work through setbacks, your social support can help to keep you accountable, provide feedback, remind you to be kind to yourself, and serve as motivators. In addition, if you know people who are persevering toward their own goals, they can set an inspiring example to help you see your journey as manageable.

WHO SUPPORTS YOUR SELF-GROWTH?

Make a row for each personal growth goal you created earlier in this chapter. In each section, list the people who you know you can count on to support you in the given goal in the column to the right. You can list someone for more than one goal if applicable.

GOAL	PEOPLE WHO SUPPORT YOU

How do you know when you can count on someone to support your self-growth?

Did you list someone more than once? What does that tell you?

Did you list someone only once? What does that tell you?

It is healthy for support to be equal. Individuals who support you may benefit from your support as well. Support is a form of love. Providing support for others honors their worth, just as you wish for them to honor yours. When you care for others by supporting them, the love that you give can come right back to you and can benefit your self-loving practice.

Use the chart below to flip your perspective on social support. List each person who appeared in the chart on the previous page. Then, delve into how you know they support you, how they may need to be supported, and how you provide support for them as well.

Name	___ supports me by...	___ needs support for...	I provide ___ with support by...

Name	___ supports me by...	___ needs support for...	I provide ___ with support by...

GIVING AND GROWING

"Be the change that you wish to see in the world."

—Mahatma Gandhi

Charity is a specific method of support that improves your happiness and promotes self-love. Its benefits include an improvement in well-being, enhancements in life satisfaction, and a reduction in symptoms of mental health impairment, such as depression. When you help others, you evoke positive sentiments that improve your well-being and ability to love yourself and others. While giving to people you know has a powerful impact, you do not need to limit yourself to those who are in your support system. Choosing to pay it forward by donating or volunteering to causes that are important can be congruent with your values and help you while you help others in need.

PAYING IT FORWARD

Brainstorm ways in which you can be helpful. This can include volunteering, donating, or random acts of kindness.

Draw a ticket for each idea in the box below.

LIFETIME LEARNER

"It does not matter how slowly you go as long as you do not stop."

—Confucius

Learning is a continuous process. Obstacles will arise and setbacks are likely. However, your perseverance will allow you to see lessons in such challenges. Additionally, even when you come to the point in your path in which all of the personal goals you set in this chapter have been met, your journey will not be over. Be mindful that new paths will surface. This does not mean something is wrong, this means you are accurately rejecting the notion that perfection is the ideal. When new goals arise, infuse the pursuit with self-love. Ultimately, as a lifetime learner, you can accept who you are while continuing to learn and grow.

Beyond the goals you crafted, what areas do you believe you would like to improve your learning in?

How will you keep an open mind to new goals that arise?

Use this space to jot down new paths for growth as they arise:

MENTAL WELLNESS

In this journey of self-love you have explored the depths of who you are in order to understand how to best love yourself. In the process, you may have noticed signs of mental health distress that may have impeded your progress. Just as you may have dealt with a sprained ankle, migraines, or allergies, experiencing mental health concerns are no less manageable.

The World Health Organization asserts that mental and substance concerns are the leading cause of disability worldwide. Mental Health America highlights that one in five Americans have a mental health condition. However, mental health problems tend to be underreported as many individuals may not even know they are experiencing a mental health problem and may not seek help. Even without a diagnosis, mental health symptoms alone are distressing and warrant adequate care.

According to the Mental Health Foundation, almost three in four people report feeling so stressed that they have been unable to cope, a critical aspect in self-care and self-love. While self-love is entirely possible to achieve despite a mental health diagnosis, poor mental wellness can serve as an obstacle in your personal growth. Nevertheless, self-love can be a useful element to improve your mental health. It is important to recognize that this workbook does not substitute for mental health treatment. Depending on the level of concern, you may need to seek the help of a trained mental health professional to assist you in your healing.

SIGNS OF A MENTAL HEALTH PROBLEM

- **Mood.** Poor mood can be a sign of a mental health problem. Also, prolonged episodes of negative emotions or drastic changes can be concerning. Examples include excessive fear, consistent sadness, or prolonged irritability.
- **Thoughts.** Long-standing negative thinking can be a symptom of an underlying mental health problem. Additionally, experiencing an increase in confusion or a decrease in the ability to concentrate may be a sign of a mental health problem.
- **Habits.** When dealing with a mental health problem, an individual may be distracted and common daily habits and preferences may shift. For example, a person may experience difficulty sleeping or eating. These changes may cause a person to experience a decrease in productivity that can affect key dimensions of life, such as school, work, or family.
- **Disconnecting.** Individuals with a mental health concern may experience a disinterest in areas that previously prompted joy. For example, they may avoid positive coping and disconnect from loved ones. Even when trying to engage with others, individuals facing mental unwellness may struggle to connect.
- **Poor coping.** In an attempt to cope, individuals who are suffering with poor mental hygiene may end up turning to maladaptive coping mechanisms such as substance abuse and self-harm.

If you or someone you know needs help now, you should immediately call the National Suicide Prevention Lifeline at 1-800-273-8255, or call 911.

Do you have any of the signs listed on the previous page?

____

____

____

____

____

Mental wellness is just as important as physical wellness. How do you tend to your mental health?

____

____

____

____

____

SELF-GROWTH CHAPTER REFLECTION

BIBLIOGRAPHY

American Academy of Pediatrics. "Ordinary Sounding Expressions of Teen Angst May Signal Early Depression: Research Finds Teens Developing Depression Likely to Use Terms Such as Feeling 'Stressed' Rather Than 'Depressed,'" ScienceDaily (2017). https://www.sciencedaily.com/releases/2017/05/170504083132.htm.

Angela M. O'Donnell, *Educational Psychology* (Hoboken: Wiley, 2011).

Anglia Ruskin University. "Natural Environments Promote Positive Body Image: New Research Shows Powerful Effect of Green Spaces," ScienceDaily (2018). www.sciencedaily.com/releases/2018/01/180118114132.htm.

Anita Woolfolk Hay, *Educational Psychology* (Upper Saddle River: Pearson, 1980).

Arjen E. van't Hof, et al. "The Industrial Melanism Mutation in British Peppered Moths Is a Transposable Element," *Nature* 534, (2016) 102–105. doi: 10.1038/nature17951.

BMJ. "Nearly One-Third of Early Adulthood Depression Could Be Linked to Bullying in Teenage Years," ScienceDaily (2015). www.sciencedaily.com/releases/2015/06/150602200506.htm.

Bowes, Lucy, Carol Joinson, Dieter Wolke, and Glyn Lewis. "Peer Victimisation during Adolescence and Its Impact on Depression in Early Adulthood: Prospective Cohort Study in the United Kingdom." BMJ (2015): 350. DOI: 10.1136/bmj.h2469.

Daniels, Elizabeth A. and Aurora M. Sherman. "Model Versus Military Pilot: A Mixed-Methods Study of Adolescents' Attitudes Toward Women in Varied Occupations." *Journal of Adolescent Research* 32, no. 2 (2015): 176–201. Doi: 10.177/0743558415587025.

Dvoráková, Kamila, Moé Kishida, Jacinda Li, Steriani Elavsky, Patricia C. Broderick, Mark R. Agrusti, and Mark T. Greenberg. "Promoting Healthy Transition to College through Mindfulness Training with First-Year College Students: Pilot Randomized Controlled Trial." *Journal of American College Health* 65, no. 4 (2017): 259–67. DOI: 10.1080/07448481.2017.1278605.

Economic and Social Research Council (ESRC). "A Healthy Teenager Is a Happy Teenager," ScienceDaily (2012). www.sciencedaily.com/releases/2012/03/120302082911.htm.

Elizabeth A. Daniels et al., "Model Versus Military Pilot: A Mixed-Methods Study of Adolescents' Attitudes toward Women in Varied Occupations," *Journal of Adolescent Research* 31, no. 2 (2015): 176–201. doi:10.1177/0743558415587025.

Elsevier Health Sciences. "Teenage Risk-Taking: Teenage Brains Really Are Different from Child or Adult Brains," ScienceDaily (2008). www.sciencedaily.com/releases/2008/03/080328112127.htm.

Ferrari, Madeleine, Keong Yap, Nicole Scott, Danielle A. Einstein, and Joseph Ciarrochi. "Self-Compassion Moderates the Perfectionism and Depression Link in Both Adolescence and Adulthood." PLoS ONE (2018). DOI: 10.1371/journal.pone.0192022.

Florida Atlantic University. "Nationwide FTeen Bullying and Cyberbullying study Reveals Significant Issues Impacting Youth," ScienceDaily (2017). www.sciencedaily.com/releases/2017/02/170221102036.htm.

Golle, Jessika, Norman Rose, Richard Göllner, Marion Spengler, Gundula Stoll, Nicolas Hübner, Sven Rieger, Ulrich Trautwein, Oliver Lüdtke, Brent W. Roberts, and Benjamin Nagengast. "School or Work? The Choice May Change Your Personality." *Psychological Science* 30, no. 1 (2018): 32–42. DOI: 10.1177/0956797618806298.

Helen Y. Weng, et al. "Compassion Training Alters Altruism and Neural Responses to Suffering," *Psychological Science* 24, no. 7 (2013): 1171–1180. doi: 10.1177/0956797612469537.

"Home Page," The Art of Living, accessed October 29, 2019. https://www.artofliving.org/us-en.

H. Y. Weng, A. S. Fox, A. J. Shackman, D. E. Stodola, J. Z. K. Caldwell, M. C. Olson, G. M. Rogers, R. J. Davidson. "Compassion Training Alters Altruism and Neural Responses to Suffering." *Psychological Science*, 2013; DOI: 10.1177/0956797612469537.

International Communication Association. "Increased Time on Facebook Could Lead Women to Negative Body Images," ScienceDaily (2014). www.sciencedaily.com/releases/2014/04/140410083503.htm.

Jacinda K. Dariotis, et al. "Latent Trait Testosterone among 18–24 Year Olds: Methodological Considerations and Risk Associations," *Psychoneuroendocrinology* 67, no. 1 (2016). doi: 10.1016/j.psyneuen.2016.01.019.

Jessika Golle, et al., "School or Work? The Choice May Change Your Personality," *Psychological Science* 30, no. 1 (2018): 32–42. doi: 10.1177/0956797618806298.

John, Ann, Alexander Charles Glendenning, Amanda Marchant, Paul Montgomery, Anne Stewart, Sophie Wood, Keith Lloyd, and Keith Hawton."Self-Harm, Suicidal Behaviours, and Cyberbullying in Children and Young People: Systematic Review." *Journal of Medical Internet Research* 20, no. 4 (2018). DOI: 10.2196/jmir.9044.

Johns Hopkins Bloomberg School of Public Health. "In Teens, Strong Friendships May Mitigate Depression Associated with Excessive Video Gaming," ScienceDaily (2017). www.sciencedaily.com/releases/2017/01/170112110042.htm.

Johns Hopkins Medicine. "How Marijuana May Damage Teenage Brains in Study Using Genetically Vulnerable Mice," ScienceDaily (2018). www.sciencedaily.com/releases/2018/12/181217101747.htm.

Katie E. Gunnell, et al., "Don't Be So Hard on Yourself! Changes in Self-Compassion during the First Year of University Are Associated with Changes in Well-Being," *Personality and Individual Differences* 107, (2017): 43–48. DOI: 10.1016/j.paid.2016.11.032.

Kelly, Allison C., Kiruthiha Vimalakanthan, and Kathryn E. Miller. "Self-Compassion Moderates the Relationship between Body Mass Index and Both Eating Disorder Pathology and Body Image Flexibility." *Body Image* 11, no. 4 (2014): 446–53. DOI: 10.1016/j.bodyim.2014.07.005.

King's College London. "Why Some Teenagers More Prone to Binge Drinking," ScienceDaily (2012). www.sciencedaily.com/releases/2012/12/121203163436.htm.

Kirschner, Hans, Willem Kuyken, Kim Wright, Henrietta Roberts, Claire Brejcha, and Anke Karl. "Soothing Your Heart and Feeling Connected: A New Experimental Paradigm to Study the Benefits of Self-Compassion." *Clinical Psychological Science* 7, no. 3 (2019): 545–64. DOI: 10.1177/2167702618812438.

Larner College of Medicine at the University of Vermont. "Teen Brain Volume Changes with Small Amount of Cannabis Use, Study Finds," ScienceDaily (2019). www.sciencedaily.com/releases/2019/01/190114130855.htm.

Lifespan. "Negative Body Image Related to Depression, Anxiety and Suicidality," ScienceDaily (2006). www.sciencedaily.com/releases/2006/06/060606224541.htm.

North Shore-Long Island Jewish (LIJ) Health System. "Bullying Leads to Depression and Suicidal Thoughts in Teens," ScienceDaily (2015). www.sciencedaily.com/releases/2015/04/150427082803.htm.

O'Donnell, Angela M., Johnmarshall Reeve, and Jeffrey K. Smith. *Educational Psychology: Reflection for Action*. Hoboken: John Wiley & Sons, 2012.

Oregon State University. "Girls Receive Conflicting Career Messages from Media, New Research Shows," ScienceDaily (2015). www.sciencedaily.com/releases/2015/05/150527180954.htm.

Patricia H. Miller, *Theories of Developmental Psychology* (New York: Worth Publishers, 2011).

Penn State. "How Teens Deal with Stress May Affect Their Blood Pressure, Immune System," ScienceDaily (2018). www.sciencedaily.com/releases/2018/12/181213131236.htm.

Penn State. "Just Breathe: Mindfulness May Help Freshman Stress Less and Smile More," ScienceDaily (2017). www.sciencedaily.com/releases/2017/04/170420090204.htm.

PLOS. "Self-Compassion May Protect People from the Harmful Effects of Perfectionism," ScienceDaily (2018). www.sciencedaily.com/releases/2018/02/180221140936.htm.

Roper, Zachary J. J., Shaun P. Vecera, and Jatin G. Vaidya. "Value-Driven Attentional Capture in Adolescence." *Psychological Science* 25, no. 11 (2014): 1987–93.

San Diego State University. "More Teens Than Ever Aren't Getting Enough Sleep: A New Study Finds Young People Are Likely Sacrificing Sleep to Spend More Time on Their Phones and Tablets," ScienceDaily (2017). www.sciencedaily.com/releases/2017/10/171019100416.htm.

Sidani, Jaime E., Ariel Shensa, Beth Hoffman, Janel Hanmer, and Brian A. Primack. "The Association between Social Media Use and Eating Concerns among US Young Adults." *Journal of the Academy of Nutrition and Dietetics* 116, no. 9 (2016): 1465–72. DOI: 10.1016/j.jand.2016.03.021.

Springer. "How Bullying Affects the Structure of the Teen Brain," ScienceDaily (2018). www.sciencedaily.com/releases/2018/12/181212135032.htm.

Stodola, Diane E., Jessica Z. K. Caldwell, Matthew C. Olson, Gregory M. Rogers, and Richard J. Davidson. "Compassion Training Alters Altruism and Neural Responses to Suffering," *Psychological Science* 24, no. 7 (2013): 1171–80. DOI: 10.1177/0956797612469537.

Swami, Viren, David Barron, and Adrian Furnham. "Exposure to Natural Environments, and Photographs of Natural Environments, Promotes More Positive Body Image." *Body Image* 24, no. 1 (2018): 82–92. DOI: 10.1016/j.bodyim.2017.12.006.

Swansea University. "Young Victims of Cyberbullying Twice as Likely to Attempt Suicide and Self-Harm, Study Finds," ScienceDaily (2018). www.sciencedaily.com/releases/2018/04/180419130923.htm.

Twenge, Jean M., Zlatan Krizan, and Garrett Hisler. "Decreases in Self-Reported Sleep Duration among US Adolescents 2009-2015 and Links to New Media Screen Time." *Sleep Medicine* 39, no. 1 (2017): 47–53. DOI: 10.1016/j.sleep.2017.08.013.

University at Buffalo. "For Teens, Online Bullying Worsens Sleep and Depression: Nearly 15 Percent of High School Students Report Being Bullied Online," ScienceDaily (2019). www.sciencedaily.com/releases/2019/05/190509142707.htm.

University of Córdoba. "Bullying Evolves with Age and Proves Difficult to Escape From," ScienceDaily (2019). www.sciencedaily.com/releases/2019/03/190314111145.htm.

University of East Anglia. "The Benefits of Social Media for Young People in Care," ScienceDaily (2018). www.sciencedaily.com/releases/2018/02/180202085257.htm.

University of Exeter. "Being Kind to Yourself Has Mental and Physical Benefits," ScienceDaily (2019). www.sciencedaily.com/releases/2019/02/190206200344.htm.

University of Florida. "Exercise Improves Body Image for Fit and Unfit Alike." ScienceDaily (2009). www.sciencedaily.com/releases/2009/10/091008123235.htm.

University of Hertfordshire. "Self-Acceptance Could Be the Key to a Happier Life, Yet It's the Happy Habit Many People Practice the Least." ScienceDaily (2014). www.sciencedaily.com/releases/2014/03/140307111016.htm.

University of Iowa. "Brain Differences: Sometimes, Adolescents Just Can't Resist," ScienceDaily (2014). www.sciencedaily.com/releases/2014/09/140911124510.htm.

University of Missouri Health. "Young Women's Body Image Critical for Good Mental, Physical Health," ScienceDaily (2016). www.sciencedaily.com/releases/2016/05/160511143816.htm.

University of Otago. "Creative Activities Promote Day-to-Day Well-Being," ScienceDaily (2016). www.sciencedaily.com/releases/2016/11/161123183914.htm.

University of Pittsburgh Schools of the Health Sciences. "Greater Social Media Use Tied to Higher Risk of Eating, Body Image Concerns," ScienceDaily (2016). www.sciencedaily.com/releases/2016/05/160511102531.htm.

University of Pittsburgh Schools of the Health Sciences. "Exploring the Teenage Brain, and Its Drive for Immediate Reward," ScienceDaily (2015). www.sciencedaily.com/releases/2015/02/150214184523.htm.

University of Southern California. "Social Gaming Promotes Healthy Behavior, Reveals New Research," ScienceDaily (2013). www.sciencedaily.com/releases/2013/04/130418100154.htm.

University of Waterloo. "Self-Compassion Key to Positive Body Image, Coping." ScienceDaily (2014). www.sciencedaily.com/releases/2014/09/140929180413.htm.

Van't Hof, Arjen E., Pascal Campagne, Daniel J. Rigden, Carl J. Yung, Jessica Lingley, Michael A. Quail, Neil Hall, Alistair C. Darby, and Ilik J. Saccheri. "The Industrial Melanism Mutation in British Peppered Moths Is a Transposable Element." *Nature* 534, (2016): 102–105. DOI: 10.1038/nature17951.

Wake Forest University. "Visual Maps Use Imagery to Help Connect Personal Passions with Potential Careers," ScienceDaily (2014). www.sciencedaily.com/releases/2014/04/140414123515.htm.

Weng, Helen Y., Andrew S. Fox, Alexander J. Shackman, Diane E. Stodola, Jessica Z.K., Caldwell, Matthew C. Olson, Gregory M. Rogers, Richard J. Davidson. "Compassion Training Alters Altruism and Neural Responses to Suffering. *Psychological Science* 24, no. 7 (2013): 1171–1180. Doi: 10.1177/0956797612469537.